It's a God Thing ...
Miracle in a Cornfield

Alan Scott

PublishAmerica
Baltimore

First printing

ISBN: 1-4137-6111-9
PUBLISHED BY PUBLISHAMERICA, LLLP
www.publishamerica.com
Baltimore

Printed in the United States of America

Dedication

To ACC

You have allowed me to lead, teach, and seek the lost.
You have healed me and let me soar.
Together we have been a part of a glorious God thing.
May it continue until He returns.

Acknowledgments

To write about a God thing seems somewhat contradictory. I absolutely take no credit, but give God all the glory. The ride at Antioch truly has been a God thing, but in the middle of this God thing were great elders like Darren Helms, Dale Wilson, Mark Harlow, Jeff Jarrett, Larry Wilson, Jim Moulden, and Dave Abel. In the middle of this God thing were great staff like Keith Meece, Scott Telle, Tina Helms, Marsha Clarke, Joe Howard, Roselyn Grubbs, Brian Dimbath, Kelly Dimbath, Bethany Telle, and Mary Hartsock (who did the work of five secretaries ... thanks, Mom!).

There were people who encouraged me along the way as this book unfolded. People like Leslie Valiant and Leslie Omer helped with editing and much-needed encouragements. Great friends like David Fuqua and Alan Bubalo who kept challenging me with early morning breakfasts at Scotty's Café and lunches at Garfield's.

Without a doubt, the most help and encouragement came from my soul mate and partner, Sherry. My wife had the dubious and somewhat forced role of reading and editing each chapter as they came home one by one. With each page and each chapter, Sherry would keep my fortitude alive with a, "It's very good." Thanks, dear, for believing in me even when it wasn't so good.

My four wonderful kids need mentioning. Brooklynn, Lauren, Morgan, and Michael sacrificed some tennis time and TV time with Dad so I could be at the office writing away. These are great kids who love God and love His church. I'm glad you have been able to be a part of this God thing. May it live in your hearts forever!

Finally, to a God who makes God things realities, I humbly say thanks. You are a grand Creator and yet you somehow see fit to pour out Your blessings on a nobody pastor like me in the middle of a southern Indiana cornfield. Your care, love, and obvious hand on my life has captured my heart and life forever. During the times I feel like quitting, I quickly realize I can do nothing else but serve You. Thank you, Jesus, for saving me, and then using me to accomplish Your will. Thanks for helping my passions to mimic yours. Salvation and grace is a God thing in itself. However, in this cornfield You gave me even more. This God thing is only a dim reflection of what someday will be when we get to sit and talk about all Your God things and all Your miracles. I can't wait …

It's a God Thing ... Miracle in a Cornfield

Introduction: Definition Of A God Thing	9
1. Desperate Times	13
2. A Reluctant Pastor	19
3. Rethinking: Evangelism, Worship, Excellence, and Equipping	29
4. Community, Vision, Purpose, and Values Take Hold	45
5. What Does Sunday Morning Look Like?	63
6. Putting a Process in Place	73
7. Staffing a God Thing	85
8. A Look at Leadership Structure	96
9. Time to Build	105
10. What's Next?	113
Notes	121
Appendix	123

Introduction:
Definition of a God Thing

A God thing is a movement of God. A God thing happens only when a person or a group of people decide to take risks and let God be God. God things go beyond our human capabilities to the unimaginable dreams that only God could accomplish. With a true God thing, things happen that would normally and usually fail if God wasn't directly involved.

It's interesting to talk with or listen to people who are a part of a God thing. Nobody is quick to take the credit for anything that has taken place. Most God thing participants are afraid to take any credit, for taking credit would perhaps jeopardize the very God thing that nobody wants to end. So instead of claiming responsibility, most people placed in the middle of a God thing simply explain their circumstance by saying, "It's a God thing." They say this a lot. This becomes language that defines a movement of God.

I think God likes the phrase, "It's a God thing." After all, isn't that what much of the Bible is about? Didn't God dwindle Gideon's army down to 300 because it was all about God's power and not Gideon's? Didn't God help Nehemiah rebuild an enormous wall in just fifty-two days to prove His own sovereignty? Didn't God refuse to take away Paul's "thorn" in order to show God's strength and not Paul's?

God wants His power seen and known, and God things do just that. Whenever someone around the church incorporates "It's a God thing" into their language, I'm pointed to the source of all that has happened at Antioch Christian Church. It makes me smile every time I catch someone explaining the blessing of our church by saying, "It's a God thing." I think God smiles too.

It's important to try and grasp the concept of a God thing before I attempt to explain what has happened here at Antioch (ACC). In the ensuing pages, I will write about things like worship, leadership, excellence, evangelism, staffing, structure, and other such important tenets in the life of a church. However, let me be very clear from the very onset ... "IT'S A GOD THING!" It has been God who has empowered us, blessed us, surprised us, encouraged us, financed us, and grown us. Without God, we would have failed miserably. Without God, any success would have been, at best, a very limited, clanging cymbal that would have been unworthy to write about.

In fact, I have hesitated writing this book in fears that I would take credit and responsibility, and thus ending our ACC God thing. I have wrestled and prayed for six months before launching into this project. I want to be very careful to deflect any credit back to God for what He has done around ACC in the past several years.

For several months, my deal with God was to begin writing this book only after ACC began averaging 1,000 or more in Sunday morning attendance. Perhaps this was my fleece. Gideon needed a fleece and he was a warrior. I'm no warrior. I'm just a no-name pastor who wants desperately to know what God's will is and how I can practically give my life to fulfill it.

So I resorted to a fleece. In our first quarter after moving into a new facility, we began averaging over 1,000 in Sunday-morning attendance. The God thing was continuing, and I felt like God was giving me the green light to write.

As I write, my prayer is that the God thing will continue at Antioch, but also God things will happen in other places as a result of trying to explain His power here. As you read, remember: it's a God thing! What happened here has been a joy to be part of, a ride I wouldn't want to miss, and a tremendous display of God's mighty hand.

What follows in the pages ahead really did happen in a cornfield in southern Indiana. Sometimes ... many times ... God will use the most unlikely people in the most unlikely places to show his indisputable glory and power. In those times all we can say is, "Yea, God! It's a God thing."

1
Desperate Times

Since 1867, Antioch has been a church with vision. Somehow God has kept a stream of leaders in place who could see a preferred future and then move in that direction. For more than 130 years, leaders at ACC have been launching innovative ideas like beginning a Vacation Bible School, starting Camp Illiana (a Christian camp for kids), aggressively supporting world-wide missions, incorporating contemporary worship, relocating from a rural, gravel road to a more seeker-accessible address on a main highway, to a three-church youth ministry that pulled together kids from different churches to form one dynamic youth ministry.

The innovative, three-church youth ministry attached to ACC is where I first jumped in. I was the first PLA (Plainville, Loogootee, Antioch) youth minister. Each of these three small churches could not afford to pay for their own youth minister, but combined could finance efforts that larger churches envied. I've often wondered why churches and adults couldn't operate more along these lines and not just our teens. Hmm.

Since those meager introductions to this special church, my

sense of ACC has continually pointed to a group of leaders and people that have always wanted to move beyond themselves. Although when I became acquainted with God's people at ACC they numbered less than 100, there were more people being prayed for on a regular basis. For years Antioch kept the 18,000 unchurched people of Daviess County as a part of their prayer request within their weekly church bulletin. Southern Indiana has a church on most every street corner, and yet ACC was praying about the thousands that didn't go anywhere. Those prayers repeatedly ... perhaps naggingly ... kept knocking on God's door.

In the early 1990s Antioch became a desperate church. ACC was desperate to grow. Desperate to see young families infuse new life. Desperate to reach lost people. Desperate to impact a community that refused to drive on a country, dirt road to investigate anything that a small, old church might have to offer. As the 21st century was fast approaching, ACC was fast becoming desperate for a future. This was a church desperate to continue the work that God had started so many years ago. At this point, Antioch's Sunday morning attendance had plummeted to less than 65 people ... including kids.

There is little written but much to be said about the power of desperation. Desperation fuels church leaders to ask hard questions. The impetus for many church turnarounds and transitions has come from the depths of desperation. God hears desperate, broken, contrite people, and His hand deliberately moves within desperate, broken and contrite churches. Desperation does not necessarily signal the end, but can be a humble, powerful beginning ... as was the case with ACC.

I recall sitting in desperate, defining meetings when the pastor and elders of Antioch began making bold, declarative statements like: "If we don't do something now, we'll be dead in five years." What amazed me was the response that echoed around the table. Everyone agreed. Nobody flinched. Instead of defeat there seemed to rise up a Godly grit to figure this all out. This was more than a decision to do whatever it takes to keep the doors open. This was a prayerful resolve to seek God's specific will and ask if the ministry of ACC could powerfully continue.

Incredible decisions came out of those desperate meetings. The biggest of which was to relocate the church in order to effectively and practically begin reaching those 18,000 unchurched people that had been prayed about for years. This was a decision based on concern for others. This was a decision that took the people of Antioch beyond themselves. It would have been extremely easy for the people of ACC to hold on to their building, and cling to their 125-year-old history instead of a possible future. I suppose it would have been overtly less stressful to simply allow the church to fade into the sunset and die a theoretical death of integrity, but that was not what God had called Antioch to do.

There were some who disagreed with a decision to relocate. In a church of 65 people, any disagreement tends to wobble the leadership legs out from under you. Any church of any size would love to have 100% support of those big, crucial decisions. With a smaller church there is often little or no margin for a lack of support. In a small church, a small number can dig their heels in, fold their arms in defiance, and completely stop God-honoring initiatives. However, a vision of a preferred future had already began to unfold, and the leaders moved boldly ahead ... even though a few made it painfully obvious they would not.

Around Antioch there is an unsaid, righteous certainty about those believers who didn't want to relocate. The certainty is they WILL be in heaven. Someday we will all be together again. Someday the hard feelings, the disunity, the earthly, junky church stuff will have dissipated as we are all re-joined around the throne of our Lord. There is a healthy understanding of the secure, heavenly eternity for those Christians who left the ranks of ACC because they didn't want to relocate. There is also a greater understanding of the eternities of lost people if Antioch didn't. The risk of seekers going to hell far outweighed the heartache of a believer leaving and moving down the street to another church.

How many churches today are existing ... merely keeping their doors open ... because of the debilitating fear of long-time believers getting mad and leaving? How many big, hard, faith-filled decisions are left to die because of the dread of Christians leaving, attendance declining and offerings suffering? If only I could bottle and dispense the courage, wisdom, and faith of the ACC leaders to launch out in spite of this fear. If their passion for lost people and real fear of hell could filter into more leadership circles, I'm sure there would be more God things to write about.

When it comes to making those big, God thing, faith-filled decisions, any church of any size must struggle with two terribly hard leadership questions. First, how many Christians will leave, go to another church, but we'll see again in heaven someday if we decide to launch out? Second, how many eternities are at risk if we don't?

Occasionally I'm asked if any church can transition and grow like ACC has. My answer is a qualified yes. Most churches would prefer a quickly-jotted-down, five-step plan that would bring them back from the grips of death. I'm not sure the latest tricks, gimmicks and church growth techniques are what dying churches should be looking for. However, a church can be resurrected if it is desperate, and the people are seeking God. Yes, if their hearts have enlarged more for lost people than for themselves. Yes, if the fear of hell looms larger than the fear of a few disgruntled, saved Christians leaving. Yes, a church can transition if it's leaders are willing to make the tough decisions and move ahead in faith and uncertainty.

Antioch leaders made the tough decision that if they were going to fail, they would err on the side of lost people ... the passion and purpose of Christ. And so they plunged ahead into uncertain waters, adventure, and a bold choice to relocate. There was one older, saintly woman who had been a "lifer" at Antioch. She began to politely ask if the decision to move could be delayed until after she died. Her name was Wilma Wilson. She had been a grand matriarch of this great, solid church. She also had a son who just happened to be an elder at the time. She asked her heart-felt question to her elder-son. Larry Wilson gave a classic response by saying, "Mom, if we wait until you die to move, the entire church may be dead." Wilma's Godly yet hard-fought response was, "Then let's go!"

In the spring of 1994, Antioch took Wilma's rally cry of "Let's go!" and did. It all unfolded as a very unique Easter celebration. That day, Sunday services began in the old building to celebrate and honor the past. And then without making any national headlines, 65 men, women, and children drove into their future by driving the dusty, gravel road one last time from their old building to the new facility located near the city, on the highway, and in a cornfield. It was a new beginning ... a new building to facilitate growth and up to 200 people. It was all an obvious celebration of Christ's resurrection, and the resurrection of what had once been labeled a dying church.

From this auspicious occasion, God began to bless and answer the prayers for lost people as Antioch took up residence in its new location. Because of this new location, ACC became visible and accessible. Within two years, the 65 who left an old building quickly became 250 in a new one. Within a couple more years, further faith-filled, finance-stretching decisions were made to build additional facility space for classroom and fellowship considerations. The God thing was happening … and most everyone believed that with 250 people, God was doing far more than anyone had dared to ask or imagine. But there was more …

2
A Reluctant Pastor

During Antioch's explosive growth from 65 to over 250 in the mid 1990s, God had placed me in Atlanta, Georgia, for training. I had resigned the PLA youth ministry and in 1993 made my way to Atlanta as a worship leader and eventual church planter.

I was continually made aware of everything happening back at ACC only because years earlier I had stolen my beautiful bride away from an Indiana town called Washington and a church named Antioch. My personal aspirations, however, were far removed from anything happening anywhere in any cornfield.

I loved the city. I still do. Atlanta is where Sherry and I grew our marriage and family. It was in the wonderful Peach State of Georgia where we both turned from young, inexperienced shades of green to beginning, visible tones of maturity. God was growing us, expanding our family from one daughter to three, widening our horizons, and (with the keenness of hindsight) was training us for what lay ahead.

Sherry and I, along with our first-born daughter, Brooklynn, moved to Georgia to help an established church transition their traditional worship service into a contemporary one. The bulk of my responsibility was leading worship and being the change agent to move from hymns, piano, and organ to a full band and modern worship choruses. This was a great run for about four years. At the four-year mark, I made my first trek to the Willow Creek Community Church, in South Barrington, Illinois, to attend the Church Leadership Conference. It was at this conference that God rattled my cages concerning his church, my gifts, and lost people. I suddenly and painfully became aware that the Church was not so much about being contemporary as it was effective. I still have the fire from the very first time I heard Bill Hybels, senior pastor of Willow Creek, say, "There's nothing like the church when the church is working right."[1]

I knew I wasn't working right and the church where I was serving wasn't as well. Somehow being contemporary had begun to overshadow the need to be effective with the unchurched. I knew the mysterious sounds deep inside me were that of change brewing within. To this day I can take you to the auditorium, the section, and the very seats at Willow where Sherry and I were sitting, and we turned to each other and said, "We know what we have to do!" Talk about your redirecting and life-defining moments.

After the CLC conference at Willow Creek, I immediately went back to the leaders of the church I was serving and told them of my experience, my refueled passion, and new direction I believed my life and ministry should take. To their credit, the church leaders listened and did their best to work with and not against me.

Together, the leaders and I made the decision for me to lead a second worship service at the church. I would speak, pull together volunteers, the band, the vision, and the whole ball of wax. I was to take on a seeker's service that would help the church become more effective in reaching lost people.

This is where I began to cut my teeth on seeker-targeted ministry. It was a blast! We formed our team of believers to begin a new ministry called New Venture. We did mass mailings and marketing campaigns costing thousands of dollars that would potentially reach thousands of people. We rehearsed our first few services. We readied. We prayed. We were commissioned by the mother church, and then in September of 1996, we had our kick-off service where real, live fish—seekers—came to check things out.

New Venture shared the stage with our mother church. New Venture came alive each Sunday at 11 ... just after the 9 a.m. service of our mother church had ended. These were busy, hectic Sunday mornings. I still led worship in the early service, and then kicked into high leadership and speaking gears for our outreach at 11.

That first Sunday of New Venture was incredible. It was a time when I've never felt more envisioned, more empowered, or more alive. Our first Sunday saw close to 200 new people show up for our first service. Our core team of New Venture leaders celebrated that night with great animation. This was a thriving team ... a core of people ... who also felt envisioned, empowered, and very much alive. God seemed to be smiling on us.

There were great stories that came out of New Venture. Stories like "The Cusser." I don't believe I ever figured out this guy's name, but he was definitely a spiritual seeker with no previous church experience. After the service, he would catch me in the parking lot and compliment me on the service and my message ... in his own expletive way. "That was the best blankity-blank church service I've ever been to. This blankity church is the most blankity-blank thing I've ever seen. I'll be blanked if I'll ever miss a service. You are a blanking good preacher!" I must admit my first, initial, internal response was a self-righteous gasp. That's not what you're supposed to say about a CHURCH service! And then I realized … God had given me just what I had asked for. Seekers. Rough-around-the-edge, cussin', don't-know-how-to-dress-for-church, don't-know-hot-to-act-in-church, sinnin', addicted, divorced, unchurched seekers. My passion has not shifted since.

I can remember Judy, who came to New Venture faithfully, but for a long time went nameless because we couldn't get her to fill out an info card on Sunday mornings. We called her the wild hair-dresser lady because she was. She wore wild, colorful, spandex clothes (yes, Grandma, in church!), had funky hair, and was a beautician. Judy was a pure seeker. She had her husband Jeff and three daughters, but she had no God. Judy loved our edgy music. She loved our casual dress. She got something out of our messages. Eventually Judy and her whole family became believers. Funky, imperfect ones, but nonetheless, believers.

There were many people stories … Ada, John, Andy, Jimmy, Alison, Rusty, Angie, Melissa, Ken, Laura, Susan, and so many others. Unfortunately these thirsty seekers were not the biggest story. In December, just three months after beginning New Venture, our seeker-targeted worship service began to outnumber the attendance of our mother church. This became somewhat of a problem. New Venture's attendance of misfits had grown past the stable numbers of our birthing, mother church, but New Venture's offerings were next to nothing. The mother church essentially was paying for everything, but they weren't seeing any of these new people being incorporated into their own numbers. When asked for a timeline of when these new people would crossover from the 11 a.m. service to the 9 a.m. service, I didn't have adequate answers. My heart told me this may never happen.

This experience was an extremely hard one to muddle through. The most difficult part however, was seeing 200+ seekers being handled treacherously as the church leaders proceeded to fire me and then abruptly close down New Venture. Many people who were going to church somewhere were suddenly going nowhere. A small part of God's Kingdom had lost ground. The enemy had attacked and won. I still carry pain from this.

All of this, of which you can probably imagine, was horribly messy and only affirmed the way most seekers see the church as completely dysfunctional. I hate that. I realize the real battle was not with flesh and blood, but I did some pretty fleshy things. I said and did wrong things to the people and leaders of the mother church. Good friendships began to be severed because of things said, attitudes strewn about, and ungodly actions on both sides of the equation. All of this still hurts to this day.

Would I have done anything differently if I had it to do over? Absolutely. I wish I could go back, but my past remains as just that, my past. Rick Warren writes about how we so often seek heaven on earth, and fail to find it. God never promised heaven on earth. He guaranteed trouble. He did tell us that on earth, He would develop our character for heaven.[2] I have surmised the difficulties I went through to be appropriately filed under the heading of character development.

When the initial smoke had finally cleared from New Venture, I was left staring at the job ads wondering what I was supposed to do with my life. Simultaneously, there was a group of about 60 adults knocking on my door. This core group of people had, like me, allowed a vision of a creative church for lost people to become cemented deep into their toes. Our hearts had become enlarged for lost people and for each other. Together, we were all asking, "Now what do we do?"

We prayed, we met, we waited, and I did a personal retreat at a campground in Indiana to sort through these incredible life circumstances. It was on that retreat—through prayer, Bible study, long walks and times of worship—that the words of a Steven Curtis Chapman song began to ring in my head. The song is uniquely titled "Burn the Ships."[3]

Our small band of explorers back in Georgia had discovered new land, but now life and ministry had taken a decidedly hard turn. In the same way the Spanish explorer, Cortez, sailed to Mexico to take new territory, and then encountered seemingly insurmountable difficulties, so had we. But Cortez challenged his followers to burn the ships. There was no way they could go back home. They had come too far by faith. They had passed the point of no return. It seemed to define where God had led and defined our hearts as well. A vision had been cast which nobody believed was supposed to be buried. So with great faith and abandonment we decided to press on … to forget what was behind us and strain ahead … we decided to burn the ships.

As I write about the many highs and lows from a now-distant perspective, my heart floods with the idea of training. God had me in training. I don't like training. Who does? I despise the inevitable soreness. Training is hard, it hurts, there's pain involved, and few stick to it. I still have to drag myself to the "Y" in an attempt to train on a regular basis. I know I need to. I know how valuable training is. I am very acquainted with the agonizing necessity attached to training, and how it catapults us all to achieve and succeed. I trust and hope I will continue my training, spiritual and physical, until the day I die.

My training in Georgia eventually led me to help organize our small band of entrepreneurs and plant a new church work that we lovingly called "ACCESS Church Community." Through painstaking efforts, we derived our unique name from Ephesians 2:18 ... "For through Him (Jesus) we have ACCESS to the Father ... " What a great name for a church! I still eke out a smile anytime someone says the word *access*. It was a name and a church that absorbed and defined our lives.

ACCESS began to grow. Our second Easter service managed to attract 380 very cool, completely ungodly, wonderful seekers. What a blast it was to work with people who didn't know God but were searching for Him—sometimes without even knowing it. The stories that ACCESS afforded us were many.

There were stories like Scott and Karon. This was a talented couple who had lived together for 10 years, and traveled in a band aboard a cruise ship for several of those years. Scott and Karon came to ACCESS looking for a church to marry them. They had been rejected by several churches because they were living together, and were blown away by the love and acceptance they found at ACCESS. After their fun wedding, Scott and Karon never stopped coming to church. They eventually became the core of our band ... Scott was our drummer and Karon our bass player. More importantly, Scott and Karon became Christians and intimate partners with God and us in ministry.

Scott and Karon introduced me to Henry. Henry was a big man sporting a mean-looking goatee and had a beer in hand when we first met. He was a drinkin', marijuana smokin', guitar playin' kind of a guy who gave God limited time at an occasional Sunday mass. Scott believed Henry should be our lead guitar player at ACCESS. I didn't think there was any way. Henry and his wife, Toni, showed up one Sunday morning for church. He began playing a wicked guitar for us shortly after, and more importantly, Henry and Toni were baptized into Christ and have never looked back. Henry is now a completely transformed worship leader who leads other seekers into God's presence each week in Georgia. How cool is that? How amazing is God when we allow Him to be?

As ACCESS grew, my life seemed to be soaring. I loved this church. I loved the people, the seekers, and how creatively edgy we were each Sunday in trying to reach them. I loved my house. I loved my wife, my kids, my backyard, my quaint little subdivision, the tall pine trees, the close proximity to the malls, our friends, the blooming dogwoods in spring, and Stone Mountain laser shows. I loved my life. There's a verse in the Bible that hauntingly speaks to the earthly euphoria I was experiencing ... "This too shall pass!" It did.

With a growing, young church plant, we sought out pastoral help. We needed additional staff. We wanted to hire a co-pastor to help shoulder the increasing load of ministry. Bringing so many new people to Christ was a blast. Continuing to develop and minister to these people soon became back-breaking. We had to have help.

We hired a co-pastor. He was a great guy, but our first mistake was in "selling" the seeker-targeted philosophy to our new staff person. This was a compromise we should have never made. For over a year, staff meetings degenerated into verbal rounds of juggling the pros and cons of being a seeker-targeted church. That was mistake number two. Our once crystal-clear vision had become muddied. Our once-united, young body of believers had begun to form walls and sides as to how we should do church. With all I had been through with New

Venture, I wasn't sure I had reestablished the necessary fortitude to ride this storm out. I didn't. This was one of those times when God's character development and training got extremely tiresome.

About this time, my first contact with the leaders of Antioch happened. I still had no aspirations for anything happening anywhere in any cornfield. Remember ... I loved MY life and MY church in Georgia. I loved the city. I audaciously conveyed to the Antioch leaders that I was a church planter ... a radical change agent. Why would they want me? They retorted with the intriguing idea of how they saw their 130-year-old church as a new church plant that needed a change agent. Inside I wrestled with why I would leave the possibilities of Cobb County's 600,000 to explore the mere 30,000 of Daviess County in Indiana? My conversations with the leaders at ACC stretched out over an eight-month period while frustrations at ACCESS were continuing to build.

My euphoria turned to agony. One day I could see the move to Antioch, but Sherry couldn't. On another day Sherry was seeing it, but I was insistent we should stay put. It was my older brother Greg who advised me that when Sherry and I landed on the same page with some amount of peace, that's when we would have some insight as to what God would have us do.

My reluctance with Antioch caused us to say no three times. The third time was even after a formal, congregational vote. It was after the third no that Sherry and I landed on the same page and decided to make the move. The only problem was that we said no after a 94% approval vote. We had effectively spit in the face of the kind people at ACC. I began daydreaming about those nasty job ads once again.

After a couple rough meetings, the leaders of ACC decided they still wanted to bring me on as senior pastor. During one of those meetings, the chairman of the board calmly looked me in the eye and said, "I don't think you deserve to come to Antioch. But if everyone thinks you should, I'll agree too. I'll support you." What a great way to begin a pastoral relationship with fellow leaders! The amazing, God thing about that man, Darren Helms, is that he has strongly supported me the whole time. Shortly after I came on staff, Darren became an elder ... and has been a man true to his word. For that I will be forever grateful.

December 12, 1999, was my first Sunday to preach at the Antioch Christian Church in Washington, Indiana. It was a long way from MY life and MY church I loved in Georgia. Maybe that was part of God's point. MY life and MY church was not HIS.

I had a bit of explaining to do those first few Sundays at ACC. I had to tearfully share my heart as to why the decision was so incredibly difficult. I had to express my deep love for the people I left behind in Atlanta ... gladly hoping to capture only half that love now in Indiana. The people of Antioch accepted me. They understood my reluctance. During those snowy holiday days of December, we decided to press on to a new year and a new beginning that was only a couple weeks away.

3
Rethinking: Evangelism, Worship, Excellence, and Equipping

One of the critical factors enhancing rapid growth at Antioch was the culture of change already in place when I arrived on the scene. From the days on the gravel, country roads to time spent in the newly relocated facility, ACC did it's best to stay on the cutting edge of ministry methodology. Antioch had gotten their noses out of the hymnals via an overhead projector and slides. The church had been incorporating contemporary worship songs into the worship services while others were fighting worship wars. ACC replaced the pews with chairs, and the overhead with a video projector. Change had become a friend to the church's members as the huge relocation project so vividly depicted.

Brian McLaren says, "Change your church's attitude toward change, and everything else will change as it should."[4] Thanks to visionary leadership, such an attitude was already in place at Antioch. The already-nurtured culture of change made my job much more pleasant … being the radical change agent that I was hired to be. However, I did test the waters with my first big "ask." I wanted to buy a set of drums to sit on the stage. We didn't have a drummer or a band, but I wanted to begin signaling what was on the horizon. It was an easy ask. Done. With elder and board approval, the red Pearl drum set became a Sunday morning fixture even though nobody was playing it. Within two months, our first worship band was up and running and the low thud of the kick drum began to be understood as the momentum of change.

I also reinforced the idea of constant change and fluidity by preaching in jeans. It feels a bit trite even writing about this, but the strategy and purpose behind this change has been huge. In the same way the church had become practical and accessible through relocation, I wanted to do the same by what I wore on Sunday mornings. A few suit and tie lovers struggled, but for the most part, my casual dress began to enhance an accepting atmosphere that encouraged people to come to church seeking God and not fearing fashion approval. I had so many people who would approach me and say, "I feel I can talk to you. You're not like other preachers." I believed it was the jeans! Others would tell me they had invited a friend to church only to hear their excuse of having nothing to wear. When it was explained the pastor wore jeans, the invited friend decided to give the church a try. The jeans reflected a culture of change that was effective and continued the momentum.

I do realize the arguments against wearing jeans to church. Trust me, I am all too familiar with the arguments. "You're not giving God your best. God deserves better than our jeans." However, I believe God wants us to be effective. I trust we are to use all means and methods possible to bring down religious defenses ... without compromising the dangerous message of Christ. THIS is giving God our best! Wearing jeans is a counter-offensive attack against the enemy who uses all means in his power to tear apart God's Kingdom. If it works, why wouldn't I wear jeans? I did. I do. It works. And the atmosphere around Antioch signals we are a different, ever-changing church that exists for those who aren't yet members.

If a culture of change wasn't already in place at ACC, I would have developed an initial message series to cultivate such an idea. Many leaders and pastors have tried to change the carpet, the music, and the order of worship, only to face dire consequences ending in complete exhaustion. The problem is NOT the changes themselves, but rather the reality of change not being viewed as Godly. So often, change is not viewed as a friend and a constant need for a growing, effective church. My fear is that many churches are stuck in a time warp simply because of the lack of teaching concerning a theology of change. Erwin McManus suggests, "Although change is rarely taught or extracted from the Scriptures, the Scriptures are a document about change."[5]

If a culture of change had been neglected before I came to Antioch, a four-week series on change in the Bible, how God changed my life, the power of change, and the necessity of change would have been a part of the preaching calendar early on.

Because the well of change had already been adequately primed, I could move beyond philosophy to specific methodology. Within my first full month of preaching, I proceeded to teach about "Redefining the Church" and focused on hot buttons like evangelism, worship, excellence, and equipping through spiritual giftedness.

Concerning evangelism, the hearts of Antioch were already soft and pliable. Remember, this was a church that for years prayed specifically for the thousands of unchurched people in the county. This was a church willing to pay the price of relocating just to add more to God's Kingdom. The focus with evangelism naturally shifted to how we would practically reach more seekers for Christ.

Everyone at Antioch agreed to strike a collective deal that went something like this: Let's build relational bridges to people, get the courage and knowledge to say something to them about Christ, and then use our seeker-targeted services on Sundays as an effective evangelism tool in our individual tool boxes. In chapter five we will explore in detail what our Sunday mornings services looked like, but in general our goal was to remove any walls or stereotypical ideas that most seekers have in coming into a church environment. Our goal is for seekers to come into a comfortable, creative, relevant setting so they can be blown away with the uncompromising, dangerous message of Jesus.

This was our agreement: get to know the waitress or cashier, say something to them, and then bring them to church. Lee Strobel notes, "That's kingdom teamwork! People praying, people building relationships with unbelievers, people using their spiritual gifts to create seeker-targeted services or events—it's a divine conspiracy to reach Unchurched Harry and Mary!"[6]

During this time of teaching through creative, powerful evangelism, God allowed me to be part of an incredible, real-life illustration that became a benchmark of evangelism for Antioch. This story began to unfold as church members kept bending my ear about a possible guitar player named Joe Howard. Joe was being heralded as one of the best musicians in town, and many were wondering if he could help get our worship band off the ground. I was open to any and all ideas.

As I began to investigate the possibilities concerning Joe, I soon discovered the colorful life surrounding this man. He had once traveled with an LA-based band opening for the rock group, KISS. Joe was a tattooed, former drug-using, alcoholic, seasoned musician who loved to rock. He worked in a factory to afford him the opportunity to play in clubs and bars on the weekends. I finally met Joe when he and his wife Angie showed up at a Bible study one cold night in January. He told me his band was playing on Saturday night at a local bar, and invited me to come check things out. I said I'd be there, and then scrambled to figure out how I could figure it out.

I called the elders and asked if they would go with me to a bar to hear Joe and his band play. I was one month into my new ministry at ACC, and I was asking the elders to go bar hopping to hear rock and roll in a place called Woody's. Incredibly, they said yes!

We prayed before we went into the bar. Once inside we all sat at a round table like ducks out of water listening to music that we weren't sure we were allowed to enjoy. Not knowing exactly how to behave in this unfamiliar territory, I can remember how we nervously kept ordering and drinking as many Coca Colas as possible!

At midnight, Joe grabbed a microphone and announced to the very inebriated crowd about the new pastor of Antioch Christian Church being in the house. The crowd responded with a brief but surprisingly spiritual "Uuuughahhhh," and then resumed it's former party state of being. Joe then surprised me by saying, "Antioch is thinking about having a band, and I might start playing with them. You should all check it out." That's when it hit me ... What just happened? At midnight in a bar ... in a small town in southern Indiana ... I had been introduced as the new pastor in town, a crowd of fun, seeking, drunk people were invited to church, and Joe was considering playing in our worship band. How cool was that? How cool is God when we allow God to be God?

It was now very early Sunday morning ... about 12:30 a.m. The elders and I came out of Woody's bar with a spirit of celebration. We prayed and thanked God for what had just happened, and then headed home for a few hours of sleep before heading off to church. We joked about our much-needed showers so that nobody in church would be suspicious of our obvious smells.

That morning at church, I had the opportunity to teach an adult Sunday school class. My lesson came from Matthew, chapter nine ... Jesus partying with the sinners. I came completely clean about what the elders and I had done just hours earlier. We talked about evangelism and building bridges. We talked about getting outside of the church walls and rubbing shoulders with irreligious people. Everyone seemed open to these new ideas of what evangelism could be. People were getting it. But one of the best things for me was to be able to model what I was teaching. The story of reaching out to Joe at Woody's bar enabled me to live out what I was teaching ... something every pastor must do to really be effective.

The repercussions from that divinely-appointed Saturday night continue to unfold even today. Other churches, Christians, and pastors began to question my spirituality and the morality of ACC condoning such worldly behavior. Early on I decided this wasn't going to squelch any of my efforts. My target, purpose, and passion were wrapped around lost people, not other non-adventurous Christians. On the other hand, as a result of our bar-room ministry, I can name you many people, including a couple other band members, who now attend

Antioch and some who have been saved ... all of which I first met at Woody's.

My initial goal of seeing a guitar player who was lovingly known throughout the community as Joe-Joe Weekend panned out as well. Joe started playing with and leading our worship band. For two years he pulled our music and new musicians together with great enthusiasm. In his third year with us, we hired Joe as our full-time pastor of music. Complete with tattoos, funky hair, and a bend for rock and roll, Joe now leads us in worship every week. He has given his life and music over to God. He has grown so much and continues to grow. Each week I watch him on stage and think about the visible testimony of God's grace he has become for this church and our community.

A changed life like Joe's always changes my life, and it changes the church. It changed the way we think about and approach evangelism.

Along with purposeful directions towards evangelism in those early weeks, I also targeted my teaching on worship. Sometimes ... many times ... believers feel the tension between refocusing on evangelism and, what seems to be, the exclusion of things believers hold dearly like discipleship and worship. It became important for us to focus on the priority of worship for the believer as we were also aggressively setting our targets on the seeker.

George Barna once reported how 7 out of 10 worshipers or close to 71% of Christians will walk away on any given Sunday feeling they never experienced God.[7] A majority of Christians leave church feeling like they never worshiped. Why is that?

I believe frustrated worshipers are takers. Frustrated worshipers will spew spiritual toxicity in the car ride home by saying things like, "I didn't get anything out of church today.

The message didn't do anything for me. I didn't like the music." When did worship shift and become something that we "get" instead of something we humbly "give"? That question became one of the main centerpieces for our teaching on worship.

Incredible worshipers are incredible givers. We began teaching and experiencing how people who give of themselves through singing, serving, smiling, listening, giving, and participating seldom walk away from church dissatisfied. Satisfaction in worship became dependent upon how much was given back to God, and not the song selection, thermostat, or sermon.

In addition to the dynamic of giving in worship, we redefined the players of worship. A conscious effort was made for everyone to understand how our band, singers, and worship leaders were not performing for the congregation. We made the very healthy distinction of all us being the worship performers and God being the audience. Our people on stage were prompters for all of us to perform and give to our Audience of One. With this being the case, everyone agreed that we should clap heartily during upbeat songs and offer thunderous applause after. All of this to say, "God, we love you. Thank you for all you've done. It's great to be in Your presence. We don't want it to stop." Even at the end of our services ... after the last amen is said ... Antiochers will applaud their Audience of One. This is not to tell the band they did great, or that the drama was good, or the message connected, but rather to tell God they just don't want to leave his presence and they've been changed by being in it.

With worship being more about giving and with an understanding of God being the audience, we added one more tenet to our initial teaching on worship. Worship is a lifestyle. All we do should be viewed as worship. Our worship was never intended to be limited. For some, the right setting, the right song, lots of people, and all on a certain day becomes their formula for worship. This limits worship to something done to you, in front of you ... but not by you in a 24/7 manner. It's a constant battle to remind everyone, but we try to teach people to take their worship beyond an hour on Sunday morning to their job, homes, grocery stores, and ball fields.

Many times on Sundays, the gracious people of Antioch create a special dynamic at the end of the morning's last worship song. A usually up-tempo song will conclude, and the room will begin to fill with a raucous applause. The applause begins to build in volume and rhythm. It reminds me of the rhythmic clapping of thousands before a Garth Brooks or Rolling Stones concert breaks loose. At the end of an ACC worship service, there is an excitement in the air which seems to be telling God of a reluctance to end the morning. For the past hour, the people of ACC have been worship givers and they don't want to stop ... and they won't as they now leave the building to BE the church through a lifestyle of worship.

As a renewed teaching of evangelism and worship began to take hold, the ideas of excellence were slowly added to the mix. This is one area I have to be extremely careful with. I am self-described as being somewhat of a perfectionist. I live for freshly-vacuumed carpet that has lines of perfection! Sometimes there is a fine line between perfectionism and excellence. For a practical working definition, we sunk our teeth firmly into the idea that excellence was giving God the best with the resources we have in all areas of ministry.

Ideas of excellence began to be noticed when at my first ACC Christmas Eve service I insisted that the church NOT smell like a church. I went to Wal-Mart and bought 25 plug-in cinnamon air fresheners to ensure, at the very least, that any unchurched people coming on Christmas Eve wouldn't think Antioch smelled like every other church they had been to! The pursuit of excellence and the battle with perfectionism grew from there.

Lee Strobel makes a great point when he writes, "It's important to emphasize that the pursuit of excellence doesn't mean neurotic perfectionism. Yet it does mean that the building, grounds, sanctuary, music, drama, media, and message are the best that can be accomplished given the church's level of resources and talents."[8] To make sure we didn't travel down the perfectionism road, consistent teaching from the Old Testament book of Malachi became the norm.

Malachi points to the incredulous way someone would offer a severely lacking sacrifice to a most excellent God. Malachi 1:6-14 depicts a priest who was offering a less-than-sacrificial animal for worship. This could be a sickly sheep … a sheep that had it's broken leg caught in a fence … or a sheep simply not worth keeping or eating. The priest would place this deficient sacrifice on the altar and give it to God with expectations of God saying, "Thank you for giving me something. I'm so honored that you even thought about me." But God says he doesn't accept these kind of offerings. He vehemently searches for a priest (pastor) who would close the temple (church) doors when such non-excellent sacrifices and ministry are offered. Close the doors when the best is not given. Close the doors when services are thrown together at the last minute. Close the doors when songs are not rehearsed, hallways are not vacuumed, and sermons are ill-prepared.

Growing up in my home church, I heard the story of an older lady who kept all of her used tea bags neatly in a box. Once the box was full, she sent her shipment of used tea bags to Africa to bless the socks off the less fortunate missionaries! Perhaps they were less fortunate because they were receiving used tea bags! As unbelievable as this story sounds, sometimes mediocrity makes sense to people. Why should you spend hours in preparation for a third-grade Sunday school class when only three kids will show up?

Why would you take your precious valuable time to rehearse a song for Sunday morning? You're not a professional ... nobody will care. When you have your own lawn, garden, and house to take care of, it doesn't make sense to volunteer at the church ... does it? With the economy and your sagging bank account, surely God doesn't expect you to put anything in the offering plate. You've already put your time in at the church, and now it's time for others to do the same ... it just makes sense.

Sometimes what is fast, easy, and seemingly logical is substituted for what is right, commanded and excellent. Biblically speaking, excellence is what God deserves and what we're commanded to give. Someone once said, "What we give to God reflects our true attitudes towards Him."

At Antioch our great God and his command of excellence drive us to keep walls painted, teach creative kids lessons, plan our worship services, rehearse and memorize our music, clean our bathrooms, write and perform dramas, mow our grass, and even vacuum the carpet (which keeps the pastor very happy!).

The Bible tells us to aim (try) for perfection, and whatever we do should be done in the name of our Lord, Jesus. This is a call to excellence in every area of the church and our lives. Martin Luther King Jr. once said, "If a man is called to be a street sweeper, he should sweep streets even as Michelangelo painted or Beethoven composed music, or Shakespeare wrote poetry. He should sweep streets so well that all the hosts of heaven and earth will pause to say, here lived a great street sweeper who did his job well."[9]

We constantly tell the people of Antioch to sing, teach, clean, lead, administrate, help, cook, play, write, decorate, encourage, and love in the best ways we know how. We work at keeping our excellence bar very high because we serve a most excellent God. Sometimes for struggling individuals the question becomes what quality of lamb will be given to a God who has given his very best. People at Antioch understand the way you serve and give to God reflects how you love Him. If you would visit Antioch, you would immediately see many spots of imperfection, but you would also see passionate people who are trying to give God their best with the resources they have. God has honored this pursuit of excellence and seekers are attracted to it.

For seekers, an obvious pursuit of excellence keeps the church from being boring and predictable. Excellence fits a world that surrounds them. Excellence takes them beyond the stereotypical walls of how church used to be. Excellence removes the church cringe factor by removing singers that can't sing, sermons that don't make sense, songs stuck in the fourteenth century, and language that doesn't connect. Giving God our best raises a bar that seekers can plainly see. I've seen incredible, non-Christian musicians come out of the woodwork and begin to play at church because we raised the bar in our music ministries. Those same musicians would have remained silent in the chairs and eventually left if the music wasn't worthy of their own abilities. Simply put, excellence attracts excellence and honors God.

In trying to give God our best, it became a logical next step to shift the thinking to spiritual gifts. If, in the name of God and excellence, we wanted leaders to lead, singers to sing, teachers to teach and so on ... we needed to put the right people in the right places for the right reasons. In order to do this, we needed to teach and practice spiritual giftedness. We needed to explain how God has given each of us at least one spiritual gift, and when we combine it with our passion and personality, the church begins to hit grand slams.

To start with, I recognized the potential danger that lay ahead in teaching about spiritual gifts. In our first attempts at creating our worship band and singers, we had many people with great hearts, but little vocal ability. Case in point is one such man whom we will affectionately but anonymously call Fred. Fred loved to be up front with a microphone helping to lead worship. This is a great man with a huge heart for God. Fred's large heart for ministry was the impetus for saying yes when asked if he would consider singing. Fred is a man of God who quickly volunteers for just about anything, and is easily recruited by well-meaning ministry team leaders. Unfortunately his singing was considerably less than his heart, but singers were needed ... and how do you talk to someone about their less-than-stellar vocal abilities? This situation was a microcosm of what was happening throughout the church in areas like leadership, children's ministry, administration, and teaching. The wrong people were in the wrong places. When a church has allowed any old warm body to take up any old place of ministry, what happens when you want to correct this by putting the right people in the right places? You guessed it ... hurt feelings. We had to take new initiatives very cautiously and proceed with much prayer and teaching.

To begin teaching about how a church should operate out of spiritual giftedness, I floated the idea of the church being a living organism as opposed to an organization. Churches as organizations are destined to flounder and fail. Churches as organizations use words like *vote, elections, committees, clergy* and *lay people*. Paid ministers are supposed to do it all in organizations, and elders and deacons are elected to make sure this happens. In an organization, lay people show up each Sunday to listen and give their money. The people in the pews are spectators and so the church becomes pastor-focused instead of people-focused. Because an organizational church is focused on the pastor, the lay people transform into sermon critics. If the sermon is good, the offerings are good. If the sermons are bad, the finance committee starts to squirm. All of this is lifeless, patently unbiblical, ineffective, and part of an organizational church.

The goal for Antioch was to become a living organism. There was a need for the Body of Christ to be the Body of Christ. For this to happen, everyone needed to view each other in the light of Ephesians four and as ministers. This is why I like the title "pastor." If I am a pastor or shepherd and the people of Antioch are operating as gifted and empowered ministers, we are on the right track. However, if I am the minister and everyone else is defined as lay people, what is that? What is a lay person? Is this half a minister, or do they just LAY around because they are a part of an organization and not a living organism? The discovering and deployment of spiritual gifts would be the difference between ACC being an organizational church or a living organism.

In support of my teaching, the leaders also agreed to begin offering the "Network Spiritual Gifts" class created by the Willow Creek Community Church. Slowly but surely people began understanding their gifts, passions, and personalities. People began incorporating the various spiritual gifts into their every day language. Words like *helps, encouragement, leadership, creative communication, giving,* and *teaching* all started weaving themselves into the life of the church. People were beginning to see how the Body of Christ was intended to operate and how each person had a unique fit.

What did we do with Fred ... the guy who was struggling with singing? We asked him to explore and discover, again, his God-given gifts. He did. He discovered his passions, gifts, and personality weren't consistent with his ministry on stage with music. He found out why there had been some inner frustrations connected to the music ministry. He discovered his untapped love for kids and how his unique qualities fit nicely into our children's ministry. Fred now thrives as a volunteer with our Crazy Critter K—3rd grade class every Sunday morning. He's a great children's minister! He still sings occasionally with our Mass Praise choir. We didn't completely kick him out of our music ministry, but we did offer viable options to help him make a joyful noise in a way consistent with his abilities.

In turn, Fred's discoveries freed up space within our vocalist team. There were also people in the children's ministry who felt stuck until they discovered their gifts. As God would design it, they fit better into our music ministry, and Fred had humbly allowed this movement to be possible by deploying his own God-given gifts. When someone is operating in an area of ministry that doesn't fit with their gift package, most of the time there is frustration, and someone else doesn't get the opportunity to plug in where they should with their gifts. Fred helped us see the practicality of putting the right people in the right places for the right reasons and how everyone wins.

With a redistribution of spiritually-gifted leaders and teachers and ministers, the church began to come alive. Things started making sense. Power and effectiveness were reinstalled into ministry areas that were previously struggling along. A church once leaning towards being an organization had begun to be transformed into a living organism. We really were redefining the Church. After teaching and practicing principles attached to evangelism, worship, excellence, and equipping through spiritual giftedness, Antioch's attendance grew from 280 to over 400 in four fast-paced months. Our two Sunday-morning services were filling up and a noticeable excitement permeated our hallways each week. We would begin getting ready for our first community-wide Easter service. Expectations were high. Most were believing and praying we would attract as many as 600 people for this exciting event. But there were other ideas that had to be put into place first.

4
Community, Vision, Purpose, and Values Take Hold

As the visible growth began to take place, I remember meeting Kathy Fowler one Wednesday night. Kathy would come to church alone ... sometimes with her kids ... but mostly alone. As she heard the teaching concerning a new way to evangelize, worship, and equip, she issued a confident warning to me: "You'll never get my husband to come to church." I took this as a personal, spiritual challenge. Within a couple of weeks, Kathy's husband showed up on the back row to check things out. There were no smiles from Marston. Only fixed eyes and folded arms to make sure no indication of any approval was given. Marston had grown up in the Catholic Church but had become a C & E mass goer ... he only went on Christmas and Easter. Marston loved his cigarettes, his long hair and earring, and his Chevy 4x4 truck. He owned a local restaurant and had three boys to occasionally boast of. He was a seeker. Just the kind of person we were asking God to connect us to and help us reach.

Within a few more weeks, Marston had edged forward to the

middle seats of our auditorium to take in our Sunday morning seeker's service. The defining Sunday came when I got up to speak and immediately spotted Marston sitting in the second row on the center aisle. He was literally just a few feet away from me as I spoke, and now seemed intrigued with every word I let fly. When that service was over, Marston popped up and grabbed me before anyone else. He pointed to the stage and said, "I want to do that." After I back pedaled a bit to make sure we were properly introduced, I asked what he was referring to. "That," he said as he pointed to the stage. He wanted to sing. He wanted to be up there rockin' with the band. Marston proceeded to tell me of his former teenage life when he toured the county with his rock and roll garage band, and now he wanted to do it again.

Because we had begun to operate out of spiritual giftedness where singers would sing, I cautiously asked Marston if I could hear his vocal abilities in action. He told me to pick out a song and he would sing it. I gave him a Willow Creek original song called "Only by Grace."[10] Four years later I'm keenly aware of how that song defined Marston and what our church is trying to accomplish.

"Only God's love could bridge the distance between us. It's only by grace that I am saved. Only by grace that I am saved."

Marston blew me away when he auditioned his vocal abilities. I appropriately worked in "Only by Grace" as a part of my message the very next Sunday. Marston belted that song like only Marston can belt. Everyone knew of the life and story behind the song, but the song itself seemed to catapult the audience into a standing ovation when it was all said and done. It was only by grace we witnessed this incredible moment. It was only by grace that Marston has gone beyond religion to grab onto a relationship with Christ. In the past few years, ACC has witnessed Marston's growth, his presence on our stage, his own baptism, and the powerful day Marston baptized his boys. It all unfolded only by grace. It was another God thing.

When a life like Marston's is changed, you ask God for more.

The ball was rolling, the harvest was beginning, but how could we ensure that it would continue? What did we need to do to keep the God momentum at full steam? How would this God thing continue?

It was time for the annual leadership retreat. This was a once-a-year gathering of staff, elders, deacons, and spouses to do checks and balances within the leadership circles of the church. More than a two-day retreat, this event had the feeling of a decided advance.

I had the privilege and responsibility to steer the direction of this particular retreat. It's significant to note that while this leadership retreat was taking place, the people of ACC were back at the church participating in a round-the-clock prayer vigil. Many people were showing up at the church in 30-minute intervals to lift up the leaders and this critical retreat. These prayers made me feel exceptionally empowered as I took the reins. My goals became very aggressive as we gathered our leadership troops to accomplish the following: 1) build community, 2) clarify the vision, 3) walk away with a clear purpose statement, and 4) begin to put core values in place.

To be at the place Antioch was, there had to be some degree of relationships and community in place. To have relocated and chart substantial growth, a certain amount of spiritual friendliness had to be in place. More community and a sense of togetherness, however, was needed. There still remained elements of a traditional church structure where the loudest, most stern voice would carry the day. No matter what direction a majority wanted to take, the most vocal would determine where the church landed. This friction only caused frustrated, side conversations after meetings and a less-than-open approach when all leaders were assembled. A tangible tension was in the air whenever the leaders called a meeting.

During that first leadership retreat, we needed to have some fun. We needed to laugh together so we could lead together. We needed to stay up late playing games and talking. We needed to pray in small groups and begin to know, love, and understand each other even better. Our leaders needed to have intimate times of worship together. That's what we tried to do. We didn't completely fix the community problem, but we did make some headway. We were able to display how church leadership can function better with chairs in a circle as opposed to sitting around a boardroom table. Some beginning ideas were set in place that increased our sense of community. These minuscule changes would pave the way for us to more effectively lead by way of consensus instead of a rigid majority vote.

Within a few short months after the retreat, church attendance was starting to crash through the 450 mark, and one particular deacon was struggling with all that was happening. Previously, his one voice had been able to stifle many leadership meetings, but now it didn't seem to fit. He wasn't sure about the rapid growth. The unyielding approach he brought to the table was being edged out by the clarion call for a growing community within leadership. He and his family decided to walk away from Antioch. They were saved believers that went down the road to another church. To the credit of this former deacon, he left in a rather quiet, non-contentious manner. Someday in heaven we'll be together with this man and his family, but the leadership change here on earth opened the floodgates so the desired idea of community could expand and grow.

With some beginning and restored ideas of community taking shape, discovering God's specific vision for Antioch was a natural next step to take as we dove further into the leadership retreat. I had earlier done some internet research and found eye-opening statistics concerning the unique demographics surrounding our church. For instance, our county's population was 29,987 in 1998 and was growing by a whopping 126 each year.

Within that population, over half were under the age of 34 and a huge percentage were teens and kids. Our median age was a 35-year-old ... 66.2% had only a high school diploma, and a mere 7.6% were college graduates. Median household incomes in 2000 were listed at $29,123. Our county was suffering from a 14% poverty level, and 53% of the people didn't attend church anywhere. We began to draw a bull's-eye around our target audience. The more specific we seemed to get, the more intensity our leaders emanated. Our profile of a Daviess County seeker was a 35-year-old person who had a high school education, was perhaps hurting economically, didn't go to church, and had several kids in tow.

We reasoned if we could lock onto this seeker profile, maybe we could figure out the elements, strategies, and methodologies to reach such a person. We began to brainstorm about music, extension ministries of food and clothing, a casual dress code, the strong need for children's and youth ministries, language that would make sense, and other ways we could hit our newly formed target. Those 18,000 unchurched people Antioch had prayed for were taking shape and form right before our eyes. The possibilities were coming to life.

As our target and strategies were coming into view, our boldness to pray became quite natural. We started the idea of asking God if he would give back to us 10% of Daviess County.

"God, as you have moved and directed us, would you allow us to reach out to approximately 3,000 people?" We still pray this prayer today. We believe it can happen.

Along with our vision beginning to take flight, I wanted to put into place a purpose statement that could be cemented into the souls of each and every member. This was a hard task to accomplish. As I dove into this process feet first, my gratefulness for Rick Warren exploded. Rick has often said how he hates to reinvent the wheel. If you can learn from other people you should. Creative, foot-noted plagiarism can be ministry genius. Warren writes, "I learned a long time ago that I don't have to originate everything for it to work. God has not called us to be original at everything. He has called us to be effective."[11] I bought into Rick Warren's advice and attitude, so I went straight to his *The Purpose Driven Church* book to lead the way in writing our purpose statement.

Our purpose writing process began in a large group by asking some general yet substantial questions like: What are we driven by? Why do we exist? What is it we want to do? What is it we want to become? How are we going to do this?

After bantering these questions around in a large group, we divided our staff, elders, deacons, and spouses into 8 small groups to do a Bible discovery. Each group had their own verses to look up and then answer: Why does the church exist? What are we to be, and how are we to do it? The passages of scripture we disseminated were Matthew 28:19-20; Ephesians 4:11-16; Acts 2:41-47; Romans 12:1-8; Colossians 1:24-28; Matthew 22:36-40; John 4:21-24; Galatians 6:1-2; Romans 15:1-7; Matthew 5:13-16; and Matthew 16:15-19.

With pencils, papers, and Bibles in hand, each group went to work. The room was filled with lively conversation and anticipation. Remember, for the most part, these were seasoned church leaders who had been around the block. They had been around the Church for many years, and yet this was a fun-filled time of rediscovering the purposes of the church.

Close to half an hour had passed and most groups were anxiously waiting to report what they had found. On a large erasable board we put some 50 one-word descriptions defining the practical purposes of the church. We touted words like: *worship, sacrifice, proclaim Christ, teaching, good deeds, acceptance, celebration, encourage, unity, glorify, love, mature, prayer*, and a host of others. It was very refreshing to see, again, why the church exists and to fill the board with definition.

My delicate job was to lead in such a way that I didn't dictate what was put on the board. I wanted all of our leaders to take personal ownership of this process, but I still had to lead in order to have a finished product. I asked our leaders if all of our one-word findings could be fit into five "E" words that define the purposes of the Church. Could we somehow place all of our one-word conclusions under the headings of "Exalt" (worship), "Encourage" (community), "Equip" (ministry), "Evangelism", and "Edify" (discipleship)? We could and we did. All of our discoveries fit rather nicely into these five E-word headings. Cool. But we were just getting started.

Next, we got back into our small groups to continue this grueling, purpose-writing procedure. I challenged everyone with the idea that to truly be a Biblical church, all five "E" words must exist in practical form. According to Rick Warren:[12]

Churches grow stronger through worship.
Churches grow warmer through community.
Churches grow broader through ministry.
Churches grow larger through evangelism.

Churches grow deeper through discipleship.

Could each group now write a paragraph incorporating these five ideas into the purpose of the Antioch Christian Church? That was the task, and with a collective sigh, they went to work. Many would raise their hands and ask me tenuous questions about what, specifically, they should write. I remained rather vague in my answers because I was pushing and hoping for ownership to begin happening. My only advice was to start the paragraph with, "The purpose of ACC is to ..."

Another half-hour later, a somewhat beleaguered bunch started writing their own paragraphs on large sheets of paper that had been taped to the surrounding walls. Along with the visible struggle, I was beginning to see a bit of pride displayed. Groups were taunting each other with whose paragraph was best. The voices I heard were the wonderful sounds of ownership.

We read through each paragraph of each group, and most people thought that somehow we were done. I insisted we were only getting started, and how each group had to take their various paragraphs and boil them down to one, comprehensible, easily-memorizable sentence. Another collective sigh and the groups reformed to get to work. With this assignment, more time was necessary and given.

Here are a few of the sentences birthed from this grueling exercise:

— "The purpose of ACC is to lovingly guide a person to seek a relationship with Christ and grow deeper through praise, prayer, and encouragement in order to create a caring community that uses the Bible as its standard."

—"The purpose of ACC is to unconditionally accept and guide each person into an active relationship with Jesus and others, helping them to use their abilities to reach others for

Jesus, establishing a community that builds on everyone's abilities."

—"The purpose of ACC is to lovingly accept and encourage all people to together become a community that loves God and reaches out to others."

I remember watching a real sense of fog and frustration begin to fill the room as the groups were trying to cram all the rediscovered Biblical ideas of a church's purpose into one concise sentence. Some were wondering why we were doing this. Others were just struggling. As each group trudged through their sentences, they transferred their scribblings onto more paper that had been taped to the wall. Each group could now see what the others had written. We were close, but not yet home.

"Let's do some wordsmithing," I called as the groups came back together for the final stretch. Our last task was to write one definitive sentence that was a collective hybrid from each group's writing. We read each group's sentence and decided what phrases or words we liked best and why. Everyone gravitated to words like: *unconditional*, *accept*, *guide*, and *relationship*. I made a strong leadership push for one of my favorite, purpose-statement words ... *relevant*. This was a word we had incorporated in the purpose statement of the church we had planted in Georgia. It was a great word. I had unknowingly packed this word into my suitcase and brought it north to Indiana.

During this portion of the retreat my wife Sherry was sitting on the front row. I can remember her with a sad, lonely tear streaming down her face as the word *relevant* was not flying in Indiana. Sherry was obviously still pained from leaving ACCESS, our church plant in Georgia. We had written a clear purpose statement in Georgia. Sherry wondered why we had to write another one ... especially one without the word *relevant*.

Nobody seemed to gravitate to my word. There were some who finally admitted they weren't real sure what *relevant* even meant! As a leader, I had to make a key decision. Would I push my leadership weight around so that MY word would make its way into the final purpose statement? Or would I back off and let a new purpose statement form ... one that had the fingerprint of ownership and not the pushiness of a persistent pastor. I pushed my precious *relevant* back into my heart and allowed new heights of ownership to take center stage.

After almost two days of retreat and a simultaneous 24-hour prayer vigil, we landed on our one-sentence purpose statement. We put the final words on the board ... "The purpose of ACC is to unconditionally accept all people and guide each one into an active relationship with Jesus."

Did it say all we wanted it to? Did it include the five "E" words? We checked to make sure. "The purpose of the ACC is to unconditionally accept (Evangelism) all people and guide each one into an active relationship (Exalt, Equip, Edify, Encourage) with Jesus." This one-word sentence captured all the one-word definitions we discovered as we had reexamined the purpose of the church. This sentence used the best words from our paragraphs and sentences and somehow satisfied all. This was it. It was short, easy to read and understand. We could effortlessly memorize it and pour it deep into our souls. We liked it ... and a tired group of leaders became re-energized by what had been accomplished. Some were high-fiving. Others were simply glad we had successfully ended this long process. Our diligent work and the prayers of many had paid off.

However as the celebration began dying down, someone in the back raised their voice and asked, "Do we really mean it?" What? What kind of question is that? "Do we really mean we want to unconditionally accept all people?" This question seemed, at first, to be a wet blanket on our celebrated accomplishment. The voice in the back of the room continued ... "If the video store owner—the one with the X-rated room in the back—walks into our church, will we accept him? If homosexuals and lesbians come through our doors, will we unconditionally accept them too?"

What followed was a great discussion challenging our motives and fortitude towards bringing lost people to Christ. Did we really want to open our doors that wide? Would we be able to love each and every sinner, and yet hold true to God's word concerning sin? Everyone agreed this was the task. Everyone believed this was the vision. And so our purpose really did become our purpose. It wasn't forced on anyone by a controlling preacher. It didn't come from a vocal minority. This purpose statement had real ownership and would be easy to circulate among the others back at ACC.

It's amazing how this simple sentence has guided us over the past four years. As I finish writing this chapter, I sit in my office reflecting on the baptisms fresh on my mind from this past Sunday. One young man was brought to church by his boss. He was 20 years old, and desperate to escape a gay lifestyle. He found Jesus, grace and forgiveness at the cross, and unconditional acceptance at ACC. His baptism reminded me of how our purpose statement is being practically lived out through dramatically changed lives.

I also baptized a young married couple. These two had been coming to Antioch for months and seemed to be connecting, growing, and loving it. From the outside, all seemed well. Within the last few weeks, however, I discovered deep-seated problems that were killing their marriage and family. The husband had been involved in pornography and was caught by the wife. The wife had grown up with a horribly-formed self-esteem, and was driven further into darkness by the hellish damage of pornography. She wondered why her husband needed to look at pornography. She began to blame herself for not being good enough. Her self-worth sank lower and lower.

What happened? This couple found Jesus, grace, and forgiveness at a church that was willing to unconditionally accept and guide them. I celebrated God's purpose for this church as I plunged them both into the eternal waters of salvation. I'm reminded how our purpose statement is so much more than words on paper. It is God's specific direction and our guiding light as we build His kingdom on earth. Nobody around here takes that lightly.

The leadership retreat had been successful in initiating ideas of community, vision and purpose. Within the final, hurried minutes, we asked everyone to write down what specific things they believed ACC would bleed and die for. What values and tenets defined the Antioch Christian Church? I quickly explained that the elders would be taking several months to write ten specific values to guide and lead us into the future. These values would direct us and keep us on track. I gave a very inspiring but less than captivating spiel with which most people concluded was only asking for more busy work. To appease their new pastor, the gracious retreat attendees began handing in papers with words like: *education, children, mentoring, worship as a lifestyle, community, excellence, Jesus, the Bible, prayer, missions,* and *families.*

The retreat was most assuredly winding down with the blank stares of the over-worked volunteer leaders. They had given two days to community, vision, purpose, and values. I was out of time and energy to pound out the core values, so I closed by reiterating how the elders would take the contributed sheets of "value words" and begin writing the core values of ACC. Most yawned, wondered why this was even important, and were anxious to get home to salvage anything they could of the spent weekend.

With a few months of due diligence, the elders of ACC quietly came up with the following core values:

1. We believe the Bible is our authority and is the complete Word of God and that Jesus Christ is the Son of God through whom we are saved.
   (II Tim. 3:16; Heb. 4:12; John 1:1-3; Colossians 1:15-20; John 14:6)
2. We believe lost people matter to God and so we value spiritual seekers by aggressively and creatively reaching out to lost people in our community and around the world.
   (Luke 5:30-32; Luke 15; Luke 119:10; Matt. 18:14; I Peter 2:9)
3. We believe excellence honors God and so we do the best we can with the resources we have in all areas of ministry.
   (Malachi 1:6-14; Colossians 3:17&23; Proverbs 27:17)
4. We believe the body of Christ should be lived out in a community of acceptance, interdependence and relationships. This kind of Acts 2 community can best be seen in small groups ... where life change happens best.
   (Acts 2:42-47)
5. We believe all believers should serve with joy out of spiritual giftedness. This will allow the right people to be in the right places for the right reasons.
   (I Corinthians 12; Ephesians 4:1-16; I Peter 4:7-11)
6. We believe in a lifestyle of worship.
   (Romans 21:1; John 4:19-24)
7. We believe gifted teaching can radically transform lives, and that all Christians are expected to be in a developmental

process of discipleship that allows for devotion to Christ to be normal.

(Rms. 10:14-17; II Tim. 3:16-17; James 1:23-25; II Cor. 13:11; Colossians 1:9-10; II Thess. 1:3; II Peter 3:18)

8. We believe in the power of prayer to move the very hand of God.

(Matt. 7:7; John 16:24; Eph. 6:18; I Thess. 5:17)

9. We believe the church should be practical, open to change, and culturally relevant without compromising the message of Christ.

(Acts 15:19; Romans 1:14-115; I Cor. 9:19-23)

10. We believe in the family and strive to educate, strengthen, nurture and support God's design of family and marriage.

(Eph. 5:22-31; Eph. 6:1-4; I Tim. 5:8)

How important are these core values? They dictated the design of our new facility because we want to be culturally relevant (value #9). Our core values have pushed us to hire specific staff. We hired a pastor of small groups and a discipleship pastor (values #4 and #7 respectively). We teach the "Network" spiritual gifts class several times a year because of value #5. We employ drama, video, dance, humor, and casual dress because of value #2. We also give 8% of our offerings to world-missions because of value #2. Value #8 moved us to form a prayer team. Value #1 forces us to teach from the Bible and give Bibles away each Sunday to visitors.

Our value statements often show up at leadership meetings. Decisions and priorities are made based on these ten identity-forming statements. These values are who we are. They ARE what we would bleed and die for. We evaluate our progress or lack thereof by these values. I hit these values throughout the year as I teach. I teach through our values as a series every other year because they are our DNA as a church.

Shortly after that first leadership retreat, I can remember several people skeptically asking, "So why did we have to write all that purpose and value statement stuff? What's the purpose and value of the purpose and value stuff?" Four years later, most understand the value of value statements, and the purpose of a powerful purpose statement. Nobody wants to go back to doing church without any of the God-given tools of community, vision, purpose, and values.

The old Antioch Christian Church in Montgomery, Indiana. This location was on a country, dirt road. This is where the church met before the move onto the highway in Washington, Indiana.

A picture of the new Antioch Christian Church building in 1994. This was the original building that ACC members constructed on highway 50 in Washington, Indiana.

The newest building project of Antioch Christian Church as seen in the summer of 2003. ACC added 85,000 square feet of space under one metal roof.

5
What Does Sunday Morning Look Like?

Justin is a thirteen-year-old whiz kid. Justin first came around ACC when he was but an 11-year-old pup. Our student ministry was trying to put together its own worship band, and a guitar player was needed. Nobody knew any teenage guitar rippers, but a few had heard of a fifth grader named Justin who could jam. Would a fifth grader be welcome to play in a teenage band? If the guitar player was Justin, the answer should be and was a resounding yes! Not only did this kid rock, he drove the band with his amazing abilities and warm, laid-back personality.

In the past few years I've been watching Justin grow. I've seen him play with the teenage SOS (Sold Out Souls) band. I've seen him help lead worship in our kids areas, and I've seen him on stage with our adult teams. Justin is soaking all of this up like a junior high sponge should. He has been unleashed with his talents, and you should see his mom and dad beaming! Justin's family has found a place ... a church ... that celebrates and uses the arts, which in turn, celebrates, uses, and values Justin.

Our Sunday morning services are exciting events which

celebrate and use the arts. We have reclaimed God's ideas like painting, lighting, design, dance, singing, humor, drama, video, and music. We use many creative art forms to grab the attention of believers and seekers, and point them to Jesus. Each week as our services hit the stage, defenses come down and people's hearts are enlarged through the power of the arts. The arts grab people right where they live. Creativity within our worship services allow church and the message of Christ to become alive and relevant. However, incorporating the arts can be a most difficult task for any church to carry out. Difficulties stem from two sources. First, people associate the arts with being entertainment or Christianity lite. Second, planning for and using creative elements is incredibly hard work that requires a church to sweat the details each week.

In managing the scenario of a crusty believer believing the entertainment theory, I have so many times become exasperated. I have argued with rusty believers who grapple with the use of the arts in church because they feel people are only being entertained, and not fed, saved, and discipled. I have fought this fight so long that I have caved. I have given up, and so I say, "You're right. We entertain. You caught us red-handed." However, after admitting my guilt of entertaining, I'm quick to point out Webster's definition of entertainment: "to keep, hold, maintain or engage the mind." THAT'S EXACTLY WHAT WE TRY TO DO EACH WEEK AT ANTIOCH! Why wouldn't we? We have dynamite for a message, salvation as motivation, and a second coming to add urgency. Why wouldn't we do everything within our power to creatively engage people's minds?

What's the alternative? To be boring and lifeless? Are these the holy marks of a mature, deeper church? For many, being faithful on Sunday mornings is synonymous with being lackluster for God. I've never understood how some can turn the dangerous message of Christ into milk toast, and then call ourselves the hope of the world? When Jesus is made to be boring, someone somewhere has sinned and lost people say, "Who cares!"

For far too long I've seen Satan take far too many God-given artistic gifts and use them to propagate his own kingdom. Conversely, I've seen too many lives changed by the power of the arts to do church any other way.

Several months back, our local paper seemed to be the forum for people to shoot anonymous darts at our artistic efforts. Our very typical small-town newspaper sports a regular feature called "Speak Your Mind," which allows anyone to vent about anything without signing their name. For weeks, cowardly no-names were complaining about un-named churches that entertained, put on rock concerts each week, and encouraged such ungodly behavior as wearing jeans to church. Everyone knew the church being written about was Antioch because we had been unofficially named "The Rock and Roll" church.

The negative slamming and bantering continued until one anonymous letter stopped the topic at hand. This final note simply said, "If it hadn't been for a church that played rock and roll music and encouraged blue jeans, my husband wouldn't be going to church." Since that time, I've stopped defending the arts. Their power doesn't need my defense. Some have negatively said our church has grown because we merely entertain the masses. I say we've grown because God has shown us how to creatively and strategically connect with a lost culture. I believe this is the same thing the Apostle Paul was doing as he expounds in I Corinthians 9:19-23. The church is God's hope for the world. Why apologize for trying to be effective by using God's gift of the arts?

Incorporating the arts is also unbelievably hard work because of the details requiring holy sweat. As we were planning our first community-wide Easter service, our dreams were big. We would rent the high school auditorium and pray for large crowds of seekers to come our way. But what would that very special Easter service look like?

I pulled together a team of creative people to brainstorm ideas that would thematically surround my message of "The Graphic Reality of Peace." What songs, skits, videos, dance, and other ideas could we incorporate into our Easter celebration that would drive the death, burial, and resurrection of Jesus home in the minds of spiritual seekers? Our one-time team met and pounded out the details. We came up with a great service. Everyone walked away excited and KNOWING our goal of 600 might just be possible. What followed was a flurry of activity and excited ministry teams making our inspired Easter plans come to life. The band and singers began rehearsing. The stage team took over the decorations. The sound and lighting people kicked into high gear. Media people worked on the videos and PowerPoint presentations. The high school lobby was readied, greeters were instructed, signs were put into place, and other last minute details were handled with amazing energy. All told, there were over 120 people that were mobilized in this Herculean effort.

How many showed up on the first, community-wide Easter service at the high school? We didn't get the 600 we were hoping and praying for. 656 came through the doors. After Easter, many of those 656 kept coming to Antioch. They had been grabbed, intrigued, engaged, ENTERTAINED through the power of the arts, and were coming back for more.

Because Easter went so well, we decided to form a more

permanent planning team to pursue excellence and to integrate the arts in all our Sunday services. There were many forward thinkers expressing their feelings that every Sunday should be approached and planned in the way our Easter service was. They were right.

Initially there were about six or seven who would meet to lay out creative Sunday services. I was leading this team, and we were experiencing some limited, ground-breaking success. Because of the diligence of this team, we were able to plan services 3-4 weeks in advance. This allowed us to come up with great ideas that incorporated the arts, and then have the necessary time to prepare and implement what we put on paper.

The people of ACC began seeing the power of an eight-minute drama. Visitors would be taken by how a few amateur actors could capture a slice of real life. Most were able to see how songs fit together to drive our topic or theme deeper into the heart. The use of video and dance became artistic elements that created a real sense of anticipation as people poured into our services.

We would eventually add a third service to accommodate the new people. We unleashed three identical services at 8, 9:30 and 11 a.m. each Sunday. The arts were engaging many people, filling up seeking hearts and empty seats.

After six months of our original planning team cranking out services, I knew my time with the team was drawing to a close. They didn't need me. Most of the time I would slow things down because of my controlling interference and pesky presence. I also needed an out from the planning team because every Tuesday night required three hours that I didn't have to give. We needed someone to take and lead the planning team, but more importantly, steer the use of arts to heights not yet climbed.

Being culturally relevant and creatively aggressive in reaching lost people are ideas stemming from two of our ten core values. The arts were allowing these specific values to breath and be realized. We were at a defining point where sticking to and heating up these core values meant hiring a staff person. To do the arts thing right, a staff position became a glaring necessity. We hired Marsha Clarke as our program director.

Marsha at the time was a member of Antioch and a local bank employee. She led a calm, settled life with her husband John and their only son Ethan. The Clarke's quaint home and country lifestyle could have easily been maintained, but the quest would have been missed. Marsha had been displaying leadership and creative communication gifts within the planning team, so we extended an invitation to her for more. At first it was a real struggle. Her life had consistency and stability. Why shake it up? What if it didn't work out ... could she go back to her old job and normal life? Through much prayer and struggling, the answers eventually were that God was calling her and so was the adventure.

Convincing the entire congregation of the validity attached to Marsha's position was a one-year process. There were some who wondered why we needed Marsha. Nothing against this home-grown kid, but what would she do exactly? What is a program director? These were very fair questions. For a church in a cornfield, all this sounded somewhat unnecessary and a bit too extravagant. One year after hiring Marsha, nobody questions her heart, what she does, or why she's on staff. The levels of excellence and creativity have risen significantly as a direct result of Marsha's passion and leadership. Because Marsha was hired "within" there was no learning curve concerning vision, strategy, purpose or values of Antioch.

Those vitally important components were already in place ... she was already sold out to what we were doing ... and now she was going to be on staff doing it!

What does a program director do? That's still a fair question to someone new at Antioch. Here's how we try to answer ...

Marsha is responsible for everything that takes place on stage during our Sunday services. All songs, videos, dramas, dance, lights, stage decorations, slides, and any other use of the arts falls under Marsha's capable leadership. She leads two planning teams of about eight people each in creatively planning our services. Having two teams allows each one to rest every other week in order to restore their imaginative reservoirs.

Five weeks in advance, I give my message topics and direction to Marsha. I call these my "A to Bs." I try to give Marsha key words, phrases, and scripture to help the planning teams know where I'm headed. I also try, best I can, to figure out how people will be coming into a service or theme, and how I hope they will leave ... thus the "A to B." Giving Marsha my thoughts begins the process of incorporating creativity and the arts into our services.

Marsha usually leaves polite but demanding notes on my desk requesting my often late "A to Bs." This begins the hard work of creativity, excellence and using the arts. To be able to give monthly direction to Marsha, I have to discipline myself to layout a teaching schedule for one year. Ideas are collected and stuffed into a sermon series idea folder throughout the year. Towards the end of November I hide away to seek God's direction, consider where the church and culture are, and lay out the upcoming year's sermon series.

Laying out one year's worth of speaking topics affords me the freedom to think ahead, adjust, plan, and help Marsha do her thing. Because my year is laid out in advance, I also have the luxury to look ahead and change a series that may not be what the body at Antioch is needing. All of this can be an extremely difficult ordeal, but without it our creativity, planning and implementation of the arts would never take place.

With my "A to Bs" in hand, Marsha goes to her planning teams on Tuesday nights. These high-energy, creative dynamos spend time in prayer, developing their own community, evaluating previous services and planning a service that is approximately five weeks down the road. All of this takes three hours or more of labor and sacrifice to pull off.

The payoff is huge. Because of our extensive planning, our Sunday morning services are creatively reaching out to lost people, and we remain culturally relevant without EVER compromising the message of Jesus. From the opening prelude to the worship songs to a video to communion to a drama to a dance to the message … everything fits together in a thematic fashion that usually makes sense to those in attendance. That's what a Sunday morning at Antioch looks like. The only order poured into concrete is the God order of being creative, effective, relevant, God honoring, and life changing. Everything else is limited only to our creativity and the power of the arts.

Does all of this work flawlessly each week? No. Sometimes a skit has poor timing. The lyrics of a song are unclear. A video clip has no tie-in with the day's topic. Sometimes using the arts means taking risks that potentially can come back to bite you. In March of 2001, we were in a teaching series called "Holiness Has Nothing to Do with My Underwear." The series title was risky enough, but on one particular Sunday we were trying to communicate "Holiness and Our Bodies." Specifically, we were asking questions like: Does God really care about our physical bodies? What should our physical response to holiness be?

The planning team decided to employ the use of a video just before I got up to speak. The video was a Mark Lowry parody called "I Can Eat It All."[13] It's a funny piece about a guy who is in love with food and eating and is suffering the weightier consequences. After the services, we heard from several people who thought we were making fun of larger, horizontally challenged people. Of course, that wasn't our intent.

We were hoping this creative video would inject some humor into the uncomfortable topic at hand. It backfired. The planning team had talked about and previewed the video, but didn't see any offensive qualities. They took the risk of using a creative art form, and it just didn't work. I've threatened to write Mark Lowry to see what kind of email he has received from this video, and if he had suggestions in dealing with our weighty problem!

Using the arts is always hard and risky, but more often than not it pays off. During the summer of 2003, I was preaching through a series called "Moving In ... Lessons Learned from the Promised Land." This was a series designed to prepare ACC for our big move into a new facility. One memorably hot Sunday in July, I was speaking on the power of one; how one man's sin can have rippling effects on many. At the end of my message I asked people to take small pieces of paper and write down any ongoing sins they were struggling with. With that, the band began to play softly behind me. I instructed everyone to bring their "sins" forward and place them into glass jars. After the jars were full, a big guy in a muscle shirt came and placed all the sin-filled jars into a burlap sack. Everyone in the audience remained silent as they watched this poignant scene unfold. Placing the burlap sack on the stage floor, my muscle dude grabbed a massive sledge hammer and positioned himself over the bagged sins. The band was playing in the background, the lights were focused on the sins and sledge hammer, and with a great yell of righteous anger, the sins were smashed and the audience erupted into a resolute applause. As the applause was still ringing, the band shifted into playing "Ocean Floor" by Audio Adrenaline.[14] "Your sins are forgotten ... they're on the bottom ... of the ocean floor. Your sins are erased ... they are no more ... they're out on the ocean floor."

At that moment, nobody in the room wanted to be anywhere else. Decisions were made and lives were undoubtedly changed. It was one of those God thing moments. A holy moment. It was a moment created by God and the arts. And in that moment, I thanked God for letting us do church this way. It was so extraordinarily powerful to allow God to be God, and unleash the arts.

Moments like our sin-smashing moment can, at times, come under harsh criticism. From the jagged darts of entertaining people to the fiery bullets of trying to manufacture emotions to the hand grenade of planning the Holy Spirit right out of church ... using the arts will stir it up. To those critics I simply say: We ARE trying to creatively engage and entertain people's hearts with the message of Jesus. We DO think real emotions, not mimicked, are part of seeking God with all that we are. We BELIEVE planning, sacrificing, working and offering our best allows for the Spirit to move more impressively than simply hoping He will spontaneously show up. To someone who would criticize the arts being in church I would ask this question: What possible reason is there for not using any possible means to creatively engage lost people's hearts and give them the possibility to share heaven with us? Without at least exploring the possibilities, you may be risking eternities.

6
Putting a Process in Place

My very first Sunday as the new pastor at Antioch had numerous, unforgettable dynamics. Too many to put down on paper. One tangible event that still takes up cranial space and is worth mentioning came at the end of the worship service. Three gracious people came forward to place their membership. It made me feel extremely warm and welcome to have people joining the church on my first Sunday in the driver's seat. I stumbled with my introductions because I had never in my life met Jason, Cathy, or Jan. Along with stumbling on and fumbling their names, I offered words of encouragement, we said the confession of Christ together, and the church welcomed their newest members with vigorous applause.

The highlight of this moment happened when I watched Jason, Cathy, and Jan turn, walk back to their seats and sit back down. Something significant took place. I couldn't immediately put my finger on it, but a mental Post-it note was made. The turning, walking back, and sitting down took all of 4 seconds, but my mind had soaked it in like a winning Super Bowl catch played back in slow motion. It wasn't until the next night I understood my churning thoughts.

The elders and I met that Monday night to touch base as I was coming out of the ministry starting blocks of ACC. They were patting me on the back for a great first Sunday, and joking about even having people join the church my first Sunday out. Somewhere in the middle of the laughter, I can remember uttering a puzzling, "Yeah, but now what?"

Someone asked what I meant by my "now what," and I began a slow discourse of say-them-as-they-come questions. Now what happens? What does it mean that these three placed their membership? Do they just go and sit back down? Doesn't membership mean more than saying a few words and then sitting down? How did these people come to the place where they wanted to become members? I didn't know the answers, but knew we needed some. Everyone eventually began understanding my questions and agreed something more was needed to intentionally guide seekers into becoming believers and active members. What kind of process could be put into place to facilitate intentional progress for anyone walking into Antioch?

As discussed in chapter three, the groundwork had already been put into place to tackle evangelism more effectively. Our beginning steps of (1) building relational bridges, (2) saying something about God, and then (3) bringing them to our Sunday morning seekers service seemed an obvious 1-2-3 punch to begin our needed process. Beyond these preliminary steps to bring people into the church, we questioned what our next steps would be.

A fourth step evolved when a decision was made to have quarterly "Welcome to Antioch" lunches. These would gather new people and offer a point of contact with elders, staff and other leaders of ACC. At this lunch our agenda would include a short multi-media on the history of Antioch, an abbreviated talk-through of our core values, a time of questions and answers, a discussion of what next steps could be for those who were ready, and of course, lunch! We would hold our "Welcome to ACC" lunches after Sunday morning services, and provide everything from the food to the table service to drinks to baby-sitting. Our end goal was to meet new people, value them, educate them about the church, and point them to a path they could continue. After people come through our doors, we've found this lunch to be a critical piece in connecting with new people and encouraging them to continue our process.

Step five became the "next steps" pointed to at the "Welcome to Antioch" lunch. Step five pointed people to a series of classes designed to build on each other. The first class is the Peace Treaty class. For years I had personally used John Hendee's *A Peace Treaty With God*[15] as a tool to help believers with foundational doctrine, and prompt seekers to make initial decisions for Christ. The building blocks for our first 101 class would be found within this remarkable tool. Within the class I would have the opportunity to expound on truths such as the cross, grace, repentance, confession, baptism, sin, a covenant relationship with Jesus, and a few other critically important ideas for believers and seekers coming into the church.

I have done the Peace Treaty with an individual sitting across a kitchen table, and I have taught it in a large-class setting. Unchurched people desperately need to be educated about basic doctrine. A lost person 30 years ago would still be able to register an "eight" on the biblical literacy scale. Today, seekers and believers would hit a very weak "two" or "three" on the Bible knowledge meters. On late night TV, Jay Leno makes it laughable to hear people genuinely try to recite one of the Ten

Commandments. "God helps those who help themselves?" replies one man. Leno asks a young woman to name the four Apostles. A blank stare is the only telling answer. Could she name the Beatles? Instantly ... "John, Paul, George, and Ringo!"

People need to know what's in the Bible, and most people want to. The Peace Treaty class is always well attended, largely because people want to know for sure about things like salvation, grace, baptism, Jesus, and the cross. The Bible says in I John 5:13, "My purpose in writing is simply this: ... that you who believe in God's Son will know beyond the shadow of a doubt that you have eternal life ... " We CAN know, and the Peace Treaty class helps us to help people know. Because of this, many decisions for Christ are made. While most believers coming into our church will say the Peace Treaty class is but a scant refresher course, I think it's more. Believers walk away knowing how to actually explain the lofty concept of grace. They gain the ability to explain the significance and importance of baptism. A practical explanation of the blood of Jesus becomes a part of their spiritual tool belt. Most importantly, believers are better equipped to share their faith with those around them that need it the most.

The Peace Treaty class affords believers the opportunity to see exactly what we teach and believe doctrinally before a decision is made to officially join the church. For seekers, the Peace Treaty affords a wonderful occasion to connect with Christ. During the course of the class, believers, and seekers openly wrestle with questions like: Can a baby be baptized? Can I live a good life and get to heaven? Why is Jesus' blood so important? Do I need a priest to confess my sins too? What about once saved always saved?

Because we always have different church backgrounds

represented in the class, we always have some lively discussions. I think they are extremely healthy. In fact, if loaded questions aren't asked, I'll raise them myself just to spark these sharpening conversations. So far, nobody has left a Peace Treaty class in a storm of rage and anger because of any heated doctrinal brawls. Most everyone leaves feeling more connected to the openness and honesty of ACC. Most of our conversions and salvation decisions happen because of our Peace Treaty class.

Along with the Peace Treaty class, step five of our intentional discipleship process includes our "How to Grow" and "Network Giftedness" classes. The How to Grow class is a four-week course teaching details about Bible study, prayer, fellowship and giving. At the end of the How to Grow class, we begin introducing our membership covenant (see appendix). Our covenant is another Rick Warren, *The Purpose Driven Church* rip-off, but it works well for us and we didn't have to reinvent the wheel.

After a person takes the Peace Treaty class and our How to Grow class, we point them to the Network Giftedness class. In chapter four, we touched briefly on how this class helps us to put the right people in the right places for the right reasons. The Network class enables us to Biblically and effectively operate as the true Body of Christ.

In previous years we tried to accomplish the Network class in an 8-week time frame. By the fourth or fifth week, our numbers had dwindled to nothing. We concluded that people wanted to take this class to find out their spiritual gifts and then get going in ministry. Waiting around for eight weeks wasn't cutting it.

We narrowed the teaching material to a one-day class. From 8:30 till 5 p.m. we slammed people with Biblical principles concerning gifts, abilities, personality mixes, and passion. They got it, but with bloodshot eyes and weariness did they survive. We thought this was a bit too much as well.

Currently we offer our Network class several times a year from 9 a.m. till 12 noon ... mostly on Saturdays. This seems to be working for us. People are still discovering gifts, personality traits, and passion, and have the energy left over to explore ministry opportunities. Because we have set this class and it's principles in motion, it is so unbelievably cool to print something like this in our weekly bulletin: "We are looking for someone with a passion for kids, a structured personality, and the spiritual gift of administration to help in the kid's ministry office." For some churches this kind of announcement would be equivalent to writing in Greek. For those at ACC, the call for doing ministry right is crystal clear.

Discovering how to do ministry right is powerfully illustrated by a guy named Tom. Tom and his wife Shelley came to us unconnected to God and searching for something beyond religion. They both methodically began our seven-step process including the Peace Treaty and How to Grow classes, but stopped shy of the Network course. At that point, Tom was prematurely asked to be a part of our lighting team. His excitement and newfound enthusiasm for God prompted him to jump in without reservation. For Tom, there were some inner frustrations unknowingly attached to the lighting team. Something wasn't right.

Tom jumped back into our process and availed himself to our half-day Network class. He quickly unwrapped his top three gifts of leadership, wisdom, and administration. Tom's personality was slanted towards tasks instead of people, and more structured than not. His glaring passion was sports. He could see where his gift discoveries enlightened him as to why he was experiencing inner turmoil with the lighting team. But where was his place in ministry?

Recently, Tom became the leader of our sports team. His gifts have enabled him to recruit and organize and move forward with full-court speed. He is energized and the Body of Christ is most definitely progressing. The process is still working for Tom. He is doing ministry right.

Doing ministry right is a benefit of our Network class, but knowing each other becomes a vital component as well. The staff will nervously joke about my complete lack of the mercy gift. My top three spiritual gifts are leadership, teaching, and evangelism. Mercy is way down my list. This doesn't give me an excuse to be merciless, but most staffers don't expect huge hugs or torrential tears when they talk with me about nagging personal problems. They know I'd much rather be leading the way in reaching and teaching lost people than offering Kleenex. They know me well ... sometimes too well. Identifying each of our gifts helps us to know each other better. When we interview for a new staff position, the first question popped is always: "What are your top three spiritual gifts?" We want to immediately investigate who this person is and how God has wired and gifted them. Discovering spiritual gifts allows new people ... any new people ... to know us and for us to know them.

Our eventual seven-step process was nearing completion. Step one: Build a bridge to someone. Step two: Say something to that someone about God. Step three: Bring them to our services on Sunday morning. Step four: "Welcome to ACC" lunch.

Step five: Begin series of 101 classes. After step five, if someone stops the process, we still have accomplished much.

A person will still have been exposed to great stuff that will carry them through to their next stop on a spiritual journey.

Were any more steps needed? We added two final pieces ... Step six is joining a small group. Small groups are incredibly important to us. As God grows us larger, we must become smaller to facilitate life-changing relationships. As our numbers have kept bumping upward, we were forced to realize how not everyone needed to know the pastor, but everyone needed to know someone. We needed to become a church OF small groups and not merely a church WITH small groups.

Scott is a man in my Sunday morning men's small group. Each of us pray for our morning services in the main auditorium, and then meet back in my office at 7:15 to rev up our small group. One Sunday morning, after a challenging discussion, one man encouraged each of us to pray with our wives at least once in the upcoming week. For some this was a discipline already in place. For Scott, this was an unbelievable stretch.

Part of the issued test was coming back the next week to report how the exercise went. With that, Scott let out a hesitant sigh but resolved to go for it. One week later we were back in my office reporting. Scott anxiously wanted to report first. He had worked third shift the night before, had only been to bed for one hour, but was blatantly prompt for our early-morning small group meeting. Scott explained with great excitement how he approached his wife in bed one night and asked her to pray.

The two of them were reading, and then Trish put her book up, rolled over and was going to sleep. Scott asked the awkward, prayer-thingy question. "You want to what?" replied his wife. Pray. Scott wanted to pray with her. He could pray at the supper table with all the kids, but this one-on-one spiritual attempt with his wife was new and nervous territory.

How does a Christian wife say no to a spiritual giant wannabe husband who is begging for prayer time? You can't. As Scott and Trish grabbed hands, Scott nervously explained to Trish that this was his small group's idea (something we failed to discourage), and if she wanted to pray she could ... but she didn't have to ... unless she wanted to ... otherwise he would just pray ... and that would be about it ... and then she could go back to sleep ... because it would all be over. "Soooo, let's pray!" Scott did, and he couldn't wait to get back to small group and tell us all about it.

As Scott verbally unpacked this landmark spiritual moment, I couldn't help but think how his life was dramatically changing right before my eyes. It wasn't a sermon that did it. It wasn't a well-planned program. It wasn't a worship service that did it. Scott's growth had been rooted in the middle of a circle of men where life change happens best.

As a disciple is growing, we believe jumping into a small group MUST be an integral part of the process. The Christian life was never designed to be accomplished alone. This belief is one of our ten core values. Core value #4 states: "We believe the Body of Christ should be lived out in a community of acceptance, interdependence, and relationships. This kind of Acts 2 community can best be seen in small groups ... where life change happens best." Joining a small group represents a significant commitment from someone who wants to grow and be molded into the person God wants them to be. Someone who has boldly taken this sixth step in our process will begin to be ready for the challenge of our seventh and final one.

The seventh step takes in consideration that a person at this level has moved considerably up the ladder from when they first walked into ACC. At this point, they have accepted Christ, and they've learned more about God and themselves. They have jumped into a ministry area and a small group, and are now ready to be challenged with their giving ability.

It's an easy out for me to tell anyone that giving is more than just giving money. It's comfortable to describe giving as something we do with our time and talent ... oh, and by the way, money. However, most people usually don't get whacked out about giving time and talent away ... especially at the level of step seven. Giving their money is another story. This becomes a true test of their spiritual growth and heart for God. In practical terms, how loosely one holds onto their wallet will determine how tightly they cling to God. Stewardship ... specifically, giving money ... becomes a great way to gauge a heart, and this forms our final and seventh step.

When a new person walks through our doors ... especially a seeker ... the antennas are up and they want to see how we will handle the money thing. Most seekers are weary we are ONLY after their money. Each Sunday we make an offering disclaimer that tells seekers and visitors to ignore the offering plate as it's passed. We're not after their wallet, but we are targeting their hearts. I DO teach about money and stewardship because Jesus did. However, I try to disarm any financial defenses that a new person may have in coming to church.

During one stewardship message series, I told the audience my fears of someone new walking away believing we were coming after their cash. To break down this defensive wall, I passed out dollar bills to everyone in attendance. If anyone was getting freaked out about my message, they could keep the money. In keeping the money they couldn't, however, go out and tell anyone we were after theirs. In fact, they would have to tell people that not only did we NOT take their money, we gave them some! I also added, if a person was OK with the message, they could simply put the dollar back in the offering plate. That

Sunday I put approximately $1,000 at risk. Our finance team was a bit squirrelly about this tactic, but THANK GOD the money all came back. Whew!

Recently we initiated "joy boxes" so that we don't even pass the offering plates. People are able to give cheerfully and hilariously by placing their tithes and offerings in boxes strategically placed around our auditorium. New people are quite shocked that no guilt and no offering plates are passed under their noses. What a powerful signal that sends to our new friends!

New people coming in on Sunday morning are somewhere within steps one, two, or three of our process. They need to be diffused concerning the whole money issue. When a person has progressed to steps six or seven, they are ready to be challenged about their giving and the condition of their heart. Bill Hybels writes, "When people surrender their life to Christ, they surrender everything, including their treasures. God becomes Lord over all they have, because everything ultimately belongs to Him."[16] Hybels is describing someone well into our process and ready for the stretch of step seven.

Watching a seeker move from step one to step seven is such an incredibly rewarding deal. Their salvation is secured. Their habits have changed. Addictions worked on. Marriages improved. Purpose renewed. Their hearts have been enlarged and are able to grasp concepts like the Biblical principle of the 10% tithe. A seeker at step one usually chokes on this concept. A transformed life at step seven tests the 10% waters with great gusto, and more often than not, gets excited about the God thing possibilities related to their giving. All of this growth has been intentionally facilitated by our God-given process.

Our seven steps have been formed. 1. Build a relational bridge. 2. Say something. 3. Invite them to our Sunday seeker's service. 4. "Welcome to ACC" lunch. 5. 101 classes. 6. Join a small group. 7. Stewardship as a gauge of the heart. With a completed process, we put it into full motion.

It's not a flawless process by any means. Many times a person doesn't go through our steps in exact, precise, numerical order. That's OK. We're not serving the process, rather the process serves us as a tool to help us save, grow and change lives. Sometimes we do better on the front, evangelistic end of the process than we do on the back, discipleship end. The pendulum constantly is swinging between the real tension of what seekers are needing and what believers are wanting.

However, because we have a process, we have a game plan. We have an evaluation tool. We have answers to our questions about people like Jason, Cathy, and Jan. What does it mean when they want to become members? How did they get to this point? What do we do with them once they are members? Our process answers these very important questions and enables us to be faithful with the lives God has entrusted to us.

7
Staffing a God Thing

When the search engines of ACC were looking for a senior pastor, there were high expectations put in place as guidelines. Leaders wanted an experienced, gifted speaker who had previously led a church of 500 or more, and would champion the efforts of Antioch's rural congregation of 250. With sites set, they sifted, sorted, and prayed.

Why would they even look at me? My track record didn't compare with the elevated goals of the search team. I had limited experience as a lead, preaching pastor. My credits included leading groups of about 200 people, and I had been previously canned by a church. All indications would say, "Run!"

Because of my early youth ministry days and the PLA (chapter 2), the people of Antioch had somewhat of a shared history with me. I had married one of their own! More importantly, they knew of my abilities, passion, vision, and work ethic. Philosophically, we were all on the same page. Along with prayer, these four elements ... giftedness, passion, vision, and philosophy ... became the working essentials for bringing me and many others on staff at ACC. As you will see, the specific details of hiring each person has varied, but these four ingredients have remained steady.

As God began to grow the church, our bars of excellence, outreach and ministry were continually being raised. Subsequently, the bar for our church staff kept climbing. For those able to take on new challenges, this was a great part of the ride. For those resistant to stretching and growing, there were grave problems.

One particular minister was already on staff before I came to Antioch. He was our youth minister; a good man with a solid heart for Jesus. With growth, however, came higher expectations that he left untouched. There grew a resistance to the call for a lifestyle of ministry as opposed to getting it all done within a 9-5 time frame. We were challenging our youth minister to step it up, but our pep talks were being turned down. Our need was to move beyond ministering to a self-contained youth group of 15-20 kids, and transition to a student ministries model where larger numbers of teens were doing ministry. This wasn't happening and frustrations were growing. The problems escalated into philosophical and methodological differences pointing to an inevitable hard change.

This was a tough thing for the elders to do. Antioch had grown to over 600 people, and transitioning a staff position held fears of moving us backwards. The right call was made, and our youth minister was asked to resign. This is never an easy thing. It may be right, but never easy. Our youth minister was asked to leave less than one year after I came on staff. This created a recipe for typical junky church junk, but we muddled and led our way through it. It was still the right thing to do.

Our tendency is to let a staff conflict remain and fester. When we postpone hard staff decisions, we slip into becoming poor stewards of God's money and resources. We also create more pain because more people will try to "save" the sinking staff person. Eventually, when that staff person is let go, there is a greater attachment with the people doing the saving ... which only creates more relational havoc.

Reflecting back, I have become keenly aware of how a staff person who worked well at a 200 level may not be the one who carries the day at 600. What course do you take if this happens? You issue the challenge and take a close look at spiritual gifts and passion to determine two things: Can there be an adjustment in stepping up to greater needs? Is there a need and a willingness to shift to a different ministry area?

We've learned much from our difficult youth ministry experience. Our schooling carried us boldly into our search for the next student ministries pastor. Three months after asking one youth minister to resign, we hired Scott Telle as our new student ministries pastor. Scott's job was to make the changeover from youth ministry to student ministries.

Scott wasn't your typical candidate for a student ministries pastor. He held a degree in math from Indiana State University and was teaching courses at a nearby technical college. As we searched for our staff position through the normal venues of Bible colleges and churches, our hunt was turning up less passion and less vision than we were hoping for. Our attention was turned towards Scott; a math teacher who displayed noticeable amounts of passion and ability as a youth ministry volunteer in a sister church.

For two years, Scott successfully led ACC's transition from an inwardly focused youth group to a dynamic student ministry. However, as stated earlier, as the growth increased so did our bars of expectations. We needed to push our student ministries further and upward. Could Scott do it? We issued the challenge and he raised the bar. But there was still more that needed to be done with our teens. We knew it and so did Scott.

We looked at Scott's passions and gifts again. He still loved the teens, but he experienced a definite shift in white-hot passion and he was rapidly developing skills with media, graphics and video. We knew we needed more in our student ministries department. Did we need a full-time staff person to help with media and communications?

With continual research and study of our ever-changing culture, we determined we did need the edge of visual communications to help us gain more ground. Scott had the passion and developing gifts to help us reach into an increasingly post-modern world, and God gave us the foresight to recognize this. Scott had been with us for two years. He had faithfully served. The purpose and vision of ACC was planted deep within his soul. Instead of trashing a staff person that God had brought to us, Scott became our pastor of media and communications. We proceeded to look for God's hand in finding the next person to lead our teens.

Our growing staffing needs also included finding someone to direct efforts with small groups and discipleship. It's important to remember our ten core values mentioned in chapter four. Allowing these values to live and breath became the push in all our staffing decisions. According to our values, we expect all Christians to be in a developmental process of discipleship. Small groups go hand in hand with discipleship. We needed the right person to lead the charge in both areas. We needed a pastor of discipleship.

Providentially, Keith Meece moved into town and began attending ACC. Keith and his wife Joanne are not your typical pew sitters. They have to dig in and roll up their sleeves or they will wither and die. The Meeces (I still wonder if the plural of

Meece is mice!), did just that. They sunk their teeth into our values and strategies and became integral members of the church.

While serving voluntarily with us, Keith was holding down a program director's job at a local Christian service camp. Keith stopped and be-bopped into my office one day just to say hello. He lightheartedly asked how things were going. I smiled and replied, "Fine ... if I just had a pastor of discipleship. You interested?" Keith didn't return my smile. He let out a stress-relieving sigh and said, "Don't even go there today!" Apparently Keith was in the middle of some work-related frustrations and was thinking about a change. My flippant invitation suddenly became serious. My smile turned into a sincere dialogue of possibilities.

Within weeks, Keith was sitting down with the elders discussing his top three spiritual gifts of teaching, shepherding and encouragement. Along with his passion of helping people to grow and his outgoing personality, Keith had the mix we believed would work well at Antioch. Under the designation of pastor of discipleship, Keith would lead the charge of small groups and education (discipleship). We brought him on board with great excitement and anticipation of all God would do through Keith's life and ministry.

About a year and a half into it, Keith was becoming overburdened with controlling the reins of two full-time ministries ... small groups and discipleship. We had to get Keith some help, and looked to Brian Dimbath for reinforcements.

Brian came to us initially as a summer intern. I knew Brian from a summer camp where I've volunteered for the past 20 years. I had the opportunity to watch Brian grow up and develop from a 9-year-old camper to a 22-year-old senior in Bible college. During a week of camp and the summer of Brian's junior year, I happened to mention how impressed I was with his ministry skills. I told him I would be privileged to have him as a part of my staff someday. Within weeks of this brief conversation, Brian called to ask if I was serious or just being nice. I was serious, and we proceeded to hire Brian as a summer intern.

During that summer internship, we were able to see first-hand Brian's gifts of administration, teaching and leadership. Brian's passion was seen in working with adults and his personality was effectively structured. He served as an intern with high marks, and nobody wanted to see him go. We needed someone to lead the offensive attack towards small groups, and Brian's abilities and passions seemed to fit. He had already integrated himself into the values and philosophy of ACC by serving a successful internship. Upon graduation from Bible college and his wedding with Kelly, Brian came on staff as our pastor of small groups.

The remaining staff positions all came from within our own walls. More and more, I find this method of hiring staff very efficient and effective. As an individual grows, leads, and makes a great impact on a ministry area pointed to by our core values, considerations become necessary for a staff position. Hiring someone from within begins with the security of a person knowing and actively buying into the direction, purpose and vision of the church. When a staff person comes to us from outside sources, there is a certain amount of time that must be given to ensure everyone is on the same page theologically, strategically, philosophically and methodologically. Time MUST be given to these perspectives when a staff person comes from somewhere other than inside the church. Disaster can strike if they are overlooked.

Hiring someone homegrown enables ministry to hit the ground running very quickly. As mentioned in early chapters, we hired both Marsha Clarke, our programming director, and Joe Howard, or pastor of music, from within our own fort. We also hired a rockin' grandma as our part-time worship director. Roselyn Grubbs grew up in the Antioch Christian Church. Her father was a long-time elder. Her mother served as a leader in missions and teaching. Roselyn also married Charles, who by the way, was the minister at Antioch for 18 years. She clearly had the heart, vision, and purpose of the church sunk deep into her being. Her music and keyboard abilities were also obvious; she became a great catch to help our growing music and worship ministry. In her sixties and with five grandchildren, Roselyn champions and rocks our contemporary worship each week.

Within our children's area we hired Tina Helms. Tina is a homegrown fireballer. She has vigorously led the way with her gifts of leadership and passion for children. Together with a small army of volunteers, Tina ministers to over 300 kids each week. Three hundred kids! We could not have gone anywhere and found a better treasure than Tina. She loves loving kids. She works on being excellent and creative. She understands the direction and vision of the church and mirrors ACC's purpose throughout the children's ministry. Our kids and families are the beneficiaries of such a strong children's program. I continually encourage Tina to keep at it. If she can keep this going for 15+ years, just think what our church will look like when these kids become the leading adults! Wow! All this from a homegrown Brussels sprout named Tina.

Tina's effective leadership has translated into huge growth within our kids ministry area. Because of this explosion, we decided to bring on a homespun children's ministry assistant. We hired Brian Dimbath's wife, Kelly. Kelly wasn't exactly raised at Antioch, but Brian was already on staff and Kelly had been thoroughly exposed and initiated as to how we approach church. Her gifts, passion, vision, and philosophy were all in line with what we needed and where we were going. Some may second guess our decision to have a husband and wife on staff together. What if conflict with Brian develops? Would we have conflict with Kelly too? If Brian would move to another church, would we also lose Kelly? That would leave two huge holes. How would this affect their young marriage? Is this smart? Will there be conflicts of interest? We wrestled with all those questions too. In fact, we struggled so much that we almost missed the gem now uncovered and known as Kelly. Some may have elected to completely avoid the risks and dangers attached to spouses being on staff together. We decided to manage the risk the best we can and move ahead. In the end, we couldn't justify NOT unleashing Kelly into ministry, and God has blessed us for making the call.

Adding staff from the inside or the outside can unfold in many different ways, but the common threads point to giftedness, passion, vision, and philosophy. After prayer and God's leading, these four areas help us to put the right staff people into the right ministry positions for all the right reasons. Our willingness to give this due diligence with each staff position has been priceless. Our willingness to adjust, shift and change within our staff to meet the growing needs of the church has been a God thing as well.

Having the ability to recognize where our student ministries needed to go and how Scott's passions and abilities shifted was done only with God's help. Most churches seeing greater needs within youth ministry would simply trade in their lesser youth minister for a greater model. God enabled us to take a second look at how He was developing and growing Scott, and then adjust, shift, and change to address other needs within our church. We valued Scott. We believed God brought him to us, and we wanted to see if a change would allow him to fit better within our church. To the credit of our leaders, we adjusted, shifted, and changed to make room for greater student ministries, and to propel Scott into a needed ministry of media and communication.

We needed to adjust, shift, and change with Keith. He was completely overwhelmed by trying to manage small groups and discipleship at the same time. With some staffing modifications, we made room for Brian to take on small groups, and for Keith to fly with discipleship. Adjust, shift, and change.

Within my role as senior pastor, there have also been many alterations to contend with. My role as pastor at the 400 attendance level was different at 600 and 800 and 1,000. With the help of the elders, I slowly realized my need for change. I was killing myself and my family. At one point, I landed myself in front of a counselor because I couldn't carry the increasingly massive load on my shoulders any longer. The advice given was to adjust, shift, and change—or die.

I had to adjust my priorities and daily routine. Sermon preparation had to somehow remain a focused task requiring at least 20 hours of my time each week. To accomplish this, my office door had to close more often. At the 400 level, pop-in visits from great friends were manageable. Now at 800 to 1,000, those same visits forced me to go back to the office late at night just to keep my head above water. I was not able to sustain the same pace of ministry at 800 that I could at 400. Priorities and daily routine had to adjust and take a totally different approach.

My counseling load needed to be shared with other staff members. They didn't mind, but sometimes ... many times ... the person needing counseling doesn't want to talk with other staff. They want time with the senior Pastor. It's tough to begin limiting your counseling and open-door time. I didn't know if people of a small town would understand how I was adjusting to deal with the demands placed on me. Would they begin viewing me as some hot-shot preacher whose head got too big for his pulpit? The fact remained ... I needed to adjust, shift, and change, or die.

I had to shift some of my responsibilities to Keith. The elders made another key adjustment in staffing by moving Keith into an executive pastor position. He would decrease his discipleship role somewhat, and would take on the day-to-day management of the staff and office. He would run our weekly staff meetings. Keith would attend the board meetings. He would take on tasks and appointments that I didn't need to attend unless Keith requested my presence. Some of this was hard to let go, but I knew it was necessary in order to stay on top of my gifts of leadership, teaching, and evangelism.

My role as senior pastor has changed significantly over the past five years. I don't know everyone in the church like I used to. I am not aware of all that happens within our building on any given night. I have to trust the staff more to carry out the responsibilities of ministry. I have to lead through Keith. I have adjusted, shifted and changed with the gracious permission of leadership, and now sustainable ministry can continue to unfold within and through me.

The kindness of the people at Antioch to allow me to adjust, shift, and change cannot be overlooked either. ACCers have been gracious in NOT expecting me to be at every event, funeral, wedding, or hospital bedside. They have realized and accepted my changing role as well. They have exercised great tolerance and forgiveness when I'm not as available as I used to be. They have also become less dependent on one person to be their pastor. People have grown to rely on other staffers, but mostly on each other within the power of small groups. This has been a healthy way for the Body of Christ to be the Body of Christ to the Body of Christ. It points to the real truth of the God thing we're in the middle of. It's not about any one person. It's certainly not about the senior pastor. It's a God thing!

8
A Look at Leadership Structure

By 1999, Antioch had made great strides as a church, but there were still some traditional nuts and bolts beginning to grow a bit rusty as the church was progressing. One of the dusty elements needing fresh paint was the leadership structure.

My first taste of Antioch's entrenched, conventional structure came with my first meeting of the church board. An hour before the board met, the elders and I convened. One of my first big asks, as mentioned in chapter three, was to buy a set of drums for the church. There was much animated discussion as to why I would want to buy drums even though we had no drummer or no band. My reasoning was to plant seeds of the soon and coming changes ... that would most definitely include music. I was hired to be a change agent, and this would begin my divinely appointed work. The bottom line for this decision was the bottom line. As with most theological, eternal issues such as buying drums, the matter boiled down to finances. Was there money on hand to buy a set of drums? Silence seemed to quickly surround the table as elders went into a deep, contemplative and, I'm sure, prayerful decision mode. With faint sounds of the "Hallelujah Chorus" falling from heaven, they decided to honor my first request and buy the drums. Great! Now let's go tell the good new to the deacons at the board meeting! I'm sure they'll be thrilled ...

At the board meeting, the air was thick with tension as the monthly clash of the Titans between elders and deacons began. There was an unsaid positioning for power and a gearing up for vocal and volume prominence. Ideas were about to hit the table. Stuff would go flying towards the proverbial fan. Decisions and agendas needed to be advanced. This was a prelude to war.

Somewhere in the middle of this, the elder's bravely told the deacons that ALAN wanted to buy drums! It was stated in the form of a question ... kind of. "Alan wants to buy drums. What do you all think?" This was my first board meeting, and I didn't purposefully come looking for trouble. Suddenly, however, I was in the hot seat, or better yet, under the interrogative spot light. I made my case and sweated my way through the board's decision to appease the new pastor and buy the drums. There was a formal motion to buy the drums. A second to the motion was verbalized, and then all in favor said "Aye." The drums officially, legally, and I think, theologically, were a done deal. It was Antioch's canonization of buying a set of drums.

Wiping my battle-weary brow, my internal questions seemed obvious: Didn't the elders already approve of the drums? Why was it voted on again by the board? Can the deacons outnumber and outvote the elders? Do the elders and deacons know what their specific roles are? Are there clear lines of delineation between the responsibility of the elders and the role of the deacons? Why was there tension around the board meeting table? Weren't we all on the same team? I walked away that night knowing something had to change or nothing would be able to grow.

My flood of questions became evidence of the leadership structure issues needing attention. Three distinct concerns began to be at the center of our efforts to reform. First, new ideas became necessary to move from a structure of control to a one of growth. Second, specific roles of elders and deacons could no longer be fuzzed or questioned. Third, putting in place a mindset of change would serve an ever-growing, successful leadership structure well. We set our course and began testing the waters.

In many churches a traditional structure serves only to control. At the top of most church's organizational charts would be the elders. One step down would be the senior pastor. Below these first two tiers sits everyone else. Everyone else must run all their ideas, dreams and hopes for ministry up through the top two levels of elders and senior pastor. For some this may seem functional and perhaps Biblical. It is, in truth, what keeps most churches from growing. Such a structure of control is what keeps God's hand from blessing.

With typical church structures, control is the name of the game. If the top leadership ranks can keep their hands on everything, then everything can theoretically be kept under a safe and comfortable control. The only problem is that God didn't call us to be safe and comfortable, but rather dangerous risk takers who would expand his Kingdom. To control is to twist what real leadership is. Unfortunately, this is the choice of many churches.

For example, take Hypothetical Dianne. She was a fabulous children's ministry volunteer. She had ideas that went beyond tame Sunday schools. She had creativity and a spiritual pizzazz begging to be unleashed for the church and kids. Her ideas to change the curriculum and paint classrooms came down through personal prayer times, but they now had to go up through the defenses of the church leadership structure ... namely the elders and senior pastor.

None of the elders had much passion for little kids. In fact for some, if church could be done without kids, then heaven really would be on earth. The senior pastor just wanted to keep the kids quiet. Having a kid's ministry was merely an effective way to keep the kids out of sight and out of adult worship. With the kids promptly removed, now the senior pastor and others could concentrate on his well-prepared sermon.

Suffice it to say, there was no real voice within the leadership structure supporting Dianne's wishes to change curriculum and paint the kid's classroom walls. Because all of this change would cost money, the decision became an easy one. No. The truth was nobody within the top leadership had a heart for kids. Nobody wanted to spend money on a kid thing if they didn't have to. So to keep things under control, the underwhelmed leaders told Dianne no. They did pass along a perfunctory "Keep up the good work," but they realistically shut her down. One year later, Dianne had quit serving in the children's area. Two years later she moved on to another church hoping to use her talents and passions for a God who DID care.

Dianne's story, although fictitiously created, is a very real scenario in far too many churches. It is a story pointing to a leadership structure of control. Within such structures lies a fear of things getting out of the leader's span of control. With an unwritten goal of knowing and controlling everything, most churches begin to max out at the 200 attendance level. At this stage of growth, many people are being God directed to go in various ministry directions, and a control structure simply can't keep up. Three things can happen. 1) A church will split. Ministry gets out of control, and a leadership push to be in command raises levels of frustration. People who wanted to accomplish something will belligerently quit and go do it somewhere else. 2) Ministry is stifled or shut down as leaders try to control. 3) Leaders and members begin to drop off from burnout. They are serving a control structure. The structure should idealistically be serving them.

What's the answer? At Antioch we began to put into place a structure for growth. This was a scary thing for a leadership team functioning as control guards. With a structure shift allowing for growth, the fearful word heard was "empowerment." We would begin to test the waters of unleashing people into ministry and trusting them with decisions and initiatives … without board approval! Essentially we were deciding to empower people for ministry.

These days as questions are fired my way about Antioch's growth, I'm quick to point out the God thing. Along with that, I tend to make references to our definite shift from control to growth … from spiritual dictatorship to a Biblical empowerment. Putting ministry back into the hands of people has broadened our base for doing more ministry and impacting more lives. Structuring for growth and empowering people unclogged the ministry bottle neck that once existed in the top echelon of our leadership.

Putting in place ideas of a structure for growth was the springboard to reshape our church board. Empowerment began with defining roles of the elders and deacons. What were they unleashed to do? What was their role in ministry? To unleash others, we had to unleash our leaders.

The first thing we did was lay out nine key ministry areas within our church. Children's, Worship, Finances, Small Groups, Discipleship, Teens, Missions, Facilities, and

Involvement became our top focal points. The goal was to make sure each of these key areas had a leader leading it. With their spiritual giftedness and passions considered, we wanted the right deacons to be leading the way in each of these nine areas. With this in place, the green light was given for our elected men to be cut loose; to lead and make decisions without funneling up and through the elders and senior pastor. The details of ministry were being put into the deacon's hands and out of the elder's. Roles of elders and deacons were slowly being redefined. The deacons were to handle the details of ministry with the blessing of empowerment. The elders were to pray, keep the direction of the church on track, deal with sin issues and help manage the growing paid staff. These movements were the inaugural birth pangs of structuring for growth instead of control.

A structure designed for growth creates growth. By its very successful design, there also came a time for continued change within our leadership structure. When a structure is successful, it will continue to dictate change in order to facilitate growth.

In each of our nine selected ministry areas, there were sub-ministries. One deacon could not possibly manage or keep his hands on all the ministry teams connected to a larger area of ministry. If a deacon tried, the monster of control would be creeping back in. Deacons had to find and allow sub-leaders to take off within ministry areas. This meant more unleashing and more empowerment. This felt, to some leaders, like there was no control or accountability. To the people accomplishing ministry, it felt like ministry should ... cut loose to advance the Kingdom. More growth resulted.

With more growth came the continued need to flex within our leadership structure. Because of a successful structure for growth, ministry areas exploded and soon demanded the attention of paid-staff positions. The staff was beginning to lead most of those nine originally selected ministry areas. They too would be learning how to lead sub-ministry teams in a way that was empowering and not controlling. The success of our leadership structure had once again pushed us to restructure.

I didn't wrap my hands around what was happening until I read some thoughts from Brian McLaren in his book, *The Church on the Other Side.*" McLaren suggests, "Every newly forming church should probably plan on restructuring every time it doubles in size. Constant change is here to stay, and if current structures work well, they will necessarily become obsolete."[17]

Becoming obsolete is what our deacons began to feel. They would come to board meetings and not have much to report because ministry was happening all around them, but not particularly within their grasp of control. The church was growing and ministry was happening, but our deacons were coming to board meetings wondering why they were coming to board meetings. A once controlling board had transformed itself into an engine for growth. The traditional church board had effectively went through a metamorphosis … becoming a practical system of ministry teams enabling significant growth.

What do we do with the elected deacons and the declining church board? The deacons are still serving as Biblical deacons are supposed to. They are serving along with many other men and women who God uses to create an alive church. The church board, on the other hand, seems to be dying a slow, natural death. Recently a church leader challenged me that when the horse is dead, dismount! Perhaps it's time to dismount. Now at 1,000, we are trying to work our way through another leadership structure change. We know it won't be our last.

At one point, with where God has us, we were beginning to

gravitate towards the idea of ACC being "staff led and elder protected." With the exception of missions, facilities, and finances, all key areas of the church are under the direction (empowering, not controlling) of paid staff. Staff led and elder protected seemed to identify where we were at, but the kinks weren't all worked out. What does it mean to be elder protected? What is the changing role of our elders? Our questions, again, seem to be begging for more structural change.

Many of our elders come from a church background where elders know every detail of all that takes place within the church. This has led many elders to believe leading is equal to knowing. To let go of knowing feels like there is no leading ... and thus a question of the need for elders. Biblically speaking, we must have elders. This is not a considered option. Perhaps our struggle within the eldership is pointing to another change resulting from the success of our flexible structure. Perhaps more change inches us closer to the biblical design of elders giving up "details" and having a laser-like focus on the ministry of prayer and the Word. Precisely like the structure found in Acts 6. As these concepts begin to unfold, our arms are beginning to wrap around the idea of "elder led and God protected." This type of structure fits more into the accepted idea of the God thing happening in our cornfield. One thing is for certain, as the God thing continues and grows, our structure will forever be in a state of flux and change. The clear message to our leaders is: Buckle up your seatbelt and hang on for the ride!

Nobody has had more of a front-seat perspective to Antioch's structural change than a leader named Richard. Richard has been a faithful board deacon for a number of years, going back to the old church on a dirt road. Since I've been at

Antioch, I've made many leadership observations of Richard. He has always been first in line to make a motion, second a motion, or take a vote. He comes from a great heritage of controlling church structures. His struggle with structural change has not gone without complaint.

However, as leadership models have evolved, so has Richard. I've seen leadership growth in this man that is unmatched. He honestly struggles with new structures, what will happen to the board, and where lines of accountability and communication sit. Many of us concur with those same thoughts. Richard, however, has made it very clear … he never wants to go back.

As God helps us, Antioch will continue to approach ministry with the kind of structure that facilitates growth instead of breeding control. If a growing number of peoples lives are won and changed, we will continue to wrestle with God's will for elders, deacons and staff. We hope God will give us the fortitude to mold and remold our leadership structure as He gives us more people to minister to. If the God thing should fail to be part of our leadership structure, then it fails to be a part of our church.

9
Time to Build

For 127 years Antioch had been very comfortable with and served adequately by a facility that held 120 people on a jam-packed, people-coming-out-of-the-proverbial-woodwork Easter Sunday. In 1994, a step of faith was taken to occupy a new building at a new location; and with room for expansion that would accommodate a nearly impossible, much-dreamed-of, unimaginable number of 250 people. For the 65 people (25 of whom were kids) of ACC moving to the new location, this was an elephant's step of faith. This was risky. The fires of possibilities were fueled and ready to be lit. Small pockets of church members were eating Sunday lunch and saying, "Just think if we could fill up our new building!"

In Daviess County, Indiana, 250 people attending the same church is a feat matched only by a local Hoosier high school basketball team winning the state championship. In fact, a church with 250 people anywhere in America is considered huge. The average American church size is around 100 members, with many churches running under 50.

For Antioch, the thought of a new building being filled with

250 worshipers became the epitome of what the Apostle Paul wrote about in Ephesians 3:20: "Now to Him who is able to do more than we can ask or imagine according to His power that is at work within us."

By the year 2000, God was showing His very real power by blowing away the core group of ACC as over 600 people were now attending. Sunday lunch conversations shifted from, "Just think," to "What now?" We were herding sheep in and out of three Sunday morning services. The parking lot chaos became board meeting fodder … especially when my preaching went long and the 11 a.m. crowd had no where to go because the 9 a.m. crowd was still in their seats! Capacity fire codes were broken every Lord's Day in Jesus' name. Church growth statistics that reminded churches of going backwards at the 80% capacity mark became laughable. We were setting metal chairs up in any space we could. We were knocking out walls of classrooms to make room for our booming children's ministry. Our crowded, narrow hallways were jammed shoulder-to-shoulder with new, excited people. We brought a portable classroom onto our campus just so we could try to have a semblance of an adult Sunday School class. The fellowship hall that was created in 1997 with an expansion project was being eaten up with build-them-as-we-grow staff offices. More than what anyone could ask or imagine was happening.

I recall going to one board meeting where everyone beforehand was buzzing with our rising attendance numbers. I made the suggestion that we take out a kitchen wall and a closet to make more room for flow, fellowship and coffee conversations on Sunday mornings. Cost of my suggestion: $5,000. This was more than our weekly budget need, and besides, the walls I wanted to take out were only three years old.

The paint had barely dried!

In spite of what church growth experts will tell you, there is a spiritual adrenaline rush when you are completely maximizing your building space. When chairs are being carried in and set up at the beginning of an already packed service, EVERYONE is impacted. A full parking lot and a fire code that's out the window signals to the entire community, "Something is happening at that church!" Much of the crowded space actually facilitated more crowded space.

We continued to take out walls, remove closets for an extra corner of space, utilize the portable classroom, and bump each other in the hallways and literally in the parking lot until one fateful day.

On a revealing Sunday morning in May of 2002, we counted 20 or more people that came in our building and left. We saw people who circled our parking lot, and like a plane being rerouted, landed somewhere else that Sunday morning. We wrestled with some heavy questions. Who were these people? Did they simply go back home? Did they go to another church? When we didn't have an empty seat for them, did they lose their seat in heaven? This revelation morning was a hard one. The excitement of our growth was now tainted by the daunting limitations of our building.

I believe we did the right thing by absolutely, positively maxing out our building space. Some churches, anxious for new space, regrettably don't fully utilize the space they have. We forced ourselves to be great stewards of the building we were in. I believe God honored that. We used every room, every hallway and every storage space. We doubled and tripled the capacities our rooms were originally designed to accommodate. This approach was absolutely right. We proved our resourcefulness. We proved our stewardship. We proved our willingness and ability to go the extra mile and put in the hard work attached to serving large numbers of people. All this character building would serve us well as we would face more and bigger facility challenges in the near future.

Consistent, growing numbers pushed us to explore possibilities of construction and the finances that would be necessarily attached. We launched into a three-year capital stewardship campaign to raise money above our regular giving for an expanded or new facility. As the campaign moved ahead, so did our attendance numbers. We would meet with the architect for certain building sizes, and then our attendance would climb another 100 people, and force us to return to the drawing board.

We were growing, maximizing space, trudging through a capital stewardship campaign, preparing for a building project, and losing people on Sunday mornings who couldn't find a seat. It was decision time.

In the Fall of 2002, we made the move to our local high school auditorium. Seating capacity: 1010. Cost: $1,200 per month (and we still had a mortgage payment on our old church building!). With the high school, there would be more room for the unchurched, but we knew of the dangers of wearing out our own members at the same time. William Temple once said, "The church is the only society in the world that exists for its nonmembers." This would be true for the people of Antioch as we exhausted ourselves at the high school. We would set up and tear down. We brought in our children's ministry equipment, and then we took it back home. We decorated the stage, and then undecorated. We kept our bar of excellence very high, but the energy of our people resources began to dip dangerously low.

Looking back on our days (actually one year and one month)

at the high school, I can fondly say, "I'm glad to be out of there!" We learned much. We learned patience. We learned how hard God's work can be. We learned what people really mean when they say, "God's church is not a building." There was much more character building that took place, and we grew ... both spiritually and numerically.

It was at the high school that I decided to take our church through a 16-week series on the book of Revelation! In spite of being a seeker-targeted church and a war with Iraq making the national prophecy gurus come out of the woodwork, we made our way through Revelation and grew. This happened at the high school.

It was at the high school we had our incredible "smashing sins" moment that I referred to in chapter five. It was at the high school our big thinking towards stage decoration and lighting became a reality. It was at the high school when many people came to know the Lord. It was at the high school, lovingly referred to now as the "desert years," that God grew ACC to over 900 people.

While the high-school stint was panning out, construction back at our church campus was slowly, but surely, unfolding. We purchased an additional ten acres to add to our original eight, and to accommodate the 85,000 square-footed facility monster God placed in our lap.

It still seems unbelievable that God would take a church over 130 years old, ready to fold, uprooted and replanted in a rural corn field, hit with post-9/11 economic challenges, and then lead this same church to build a steel monster unlike anyone in rural southern Indiana had seen. Many people outside our burgeoning walls claimed we were crazy. "You just can't build a building like that," many outside crusty Christians would critically cry.

However, we remembered the prayer we had been praying, "Lord, give us 10% of Daviess County." Our rural "ciphering" pointed us to a new unimaginable number of 3,000. While many were calling us crazy, we believed our steel monster was just the right size to house HIS vision.

The story of how we got our hands on an 85,000 square foot steel structure only adds to ACC's definition of a "God thing." During our earlier, over-crowded, breaking-the-fire-codes-in-three-services days, Antioch's leadership went into a time of prayer. Corporate prayer, concerts of prayer, individual prayer ... we intentionally created a season of prayer.

As we sought God's hand, the availability of a giant steel structure suddenly became a possibility to contend with. A local philanthropist had bought and donated a steel structure to our local YMCA to build an indoor soccer arena. When it came time for construction, the generous donor had to pull out of the project because of other investments souring. Our YMCA couldn't continue the project on their own, and so we were tipped off that a large structure could be purchased at almost sixty cents on the dollar.

With leadership agreeing that God had led through prayer, we purchased the steel for $65,000. The steel had originally cost $165,000. We thanked God for immediately building $100,000 equity into our new building even before we started. More and more people were having Sunday lunch conversations about "The God thing in a cornfield."

The actual construction process was hard, and I didn't lift one hammer! We had weather delays, construction delays, state code delays, highway department frustrations, and no less than five promised and missed move-in dates. We would announce a construction company's guaranteed move-in Sunday to our high-school-weary church, and then had to eat church crow as we couldn't. Our welcome at the high school was beginning to wear thin. All parties involved believed our expected tenure at the high school would extend three to four months at the most. Ten months into it ... our much-anticipated move-in date kept being pushed back.

People tell me how normal our frustrations and experience was in constructing and finally moving into a new church building. They're probably right, but their awareness didn't make our pain any easier! Throughout the entire process, there is one decision made that I will never regret.

Early on in the construction project, I asked the elders and building teams to keep me out of the details and meetings as much as possible so I could focus on ministry. Far too many senior pastors get sucked into the draining details of buildings and neglect the ministry of the people. I was determined to keep the ministry fires alive while others were putting out the fires of construction details, delays and frustrations. If I was needed for a design or construction question that was understood. However, the thinking was to let the builders build and the preachers preach. I think that was absolutely the right decision. Sermon prep was my thing, while cement, hammers, and nails were in the hands of others. That's not just smart, it's how the Body of Christ is supposed to work.

We finally did move into our new facility on September 28, 2003. What a day that was! Most people's comments were either, "Who would believe there would be something like this in Daviess County," or "It's a God thing."

We built out exactly half of our 85,000-square-foot building. Everything is under roof, but only half is being initially used. In our first phase of build out, we completed a large atrium area, kitchen, and bookstore. In addition, we built out an auditorium with a sizeable stage to facilitate approximately 600 in one worship setting. As we move towards 1,100, we are accommodating our numbers with two Sunday morning services.

Recently in an elder's meeting, the comment was made how this building feels so much like home. Although we've only been in our building for eight months, one elder noted how it felt like we had been in for over five years. Another elder piped up and commented how small our building now seemed as our atrium and auditorium are being filled again in two services. Everyone laughed and agreed. We were labeled crazy to take risks to build such a building, but now it didn't seem so crazy … it almost seemed too small!

On our first Easter in the new building, God sent 1,600 people our way. We were blown away. There's new talk around our leadership tables. We need expanded children's areas. Adult classroom space has become an outrageous need. Our building team is reforming. We really MUST be crazy, because it feels like it's time to build … again.

10
What's Next

This is the last chapter on my first attempt to write a book. I know these last few pages are critical. With appropriate closing words, a good author wraps up his package for delivery. The last chapter is the anchor of any good book. Anyone knows this. I certainly do. It was by grabbing on to those anchors and desperately reading only last chapters that I managed to get through many college classes!

I am somewhat aware of the potential pressure attached to the last chapter. Through the power of "the last chapter," writers will, in large part, convince readers to return to the author's next book to be published.

Honestly I have no designs on a next book, but I do hope a few will read this one. With all that said, it must be overtly obvious that I am struggling immensely with this last chapter. Can you tell? Like a sophomoric attempt to stretch a 100-word paragraph into a 1,200 word English paper, I find myself rambling very, very, very, very much.

Why the struggle? Because the God thing in the cornfield continues. There is no "end" to write about. How do you wrap this God thing up nice and neat? There is no anchor to throw into the water because God is still steering this ship at full throttle. In so many ways, each week brings feelings of new beginnings and new chapters at the Antioch Christian Church. There are new people that need to become a part of our community. There are believers struggling with their purpose. Dysfunctional families and marriages continue to keep our challenge bar high. Facility and resource challenges tend to keep me awake at night and out of bed early in the morning. Additionally, with a risk-taking staff, new ideas and ministries are constantly being thrown into the mix. How do you write an ending to all of this? You don't. You can't.

However, I find myself thinking often about what's next. What will take ACC to the next levels? What will be the growth engines to fully realize 10% of Daviess and surrounding counties?

For the longest time I searched for proven, tried and even magical formulas to keep growth constant and the God thing alive. I would read the latest books recommended at the trendiest national conferences that were pointed to at the best-attended regional half-day seminars. I exposed myself to most of the well-known, growing churches in America as I hunted down what Antioch needed next. I wanted to keep the ACC God thing alive.

Reread that last sentence. Do you see the flaw? "*I* wanted to keep the ACC God thing alive." You or I can't keep a God thing alive. If we could, then it wouldn't be a God thing, would it?

Finally I did stumble onto the right book with the right stuff. It was all found in a book called Acts, and the really good church growth concepts were laid out in chapter two. God had the proven formula all along to keep HIS church and HIS God thing alive.

Through a long-distance mentoring relationship, Senior Pastor Rick Stedman of the Adventure Christian Church[18] in Roseville, California pointed me back to God's church growth principles found in Acts chapter two. Rick planted Adventure with no core members, and in 10 short, fast years God grew this incredible church to over 6,000. How did this happen and what could Antioch glean?

When Rick started this new church plant, he knew he had a limited budget, no core team, no facility, and few connections in Roseville. He conceded the fact that in the early days he wouldn't have a rockin' band, fancy lights, or PowerPoint slides like many of the other churches across town. He did, however, have a tremendous resolve to do four things well: 1) Love people one at a time. 2) Feed people God's Word. 3) Connect people to God through prayer and worship. 4) Motivate people to reach out and serve.

These four focus points formed the four-piston engine that would drive Adventure. It's the same engine that drove God's church in it's initial stages. These were the strategies the first century church employed in Acts 2, and God grew His church by 3,000 on the first day and daily thereafter. What seemed to work in Acts 2 is working in Roseville and now is taking ACC to next levels as well.

To love people one at a time, we've had to loosen our grip on the crowd and growing numbers. We are slowly learning how the unchurched don't care how big a church is, they just want to be personally loved. Having loosened our grip on the rush of increasing numbers, the focus has shifted to loving people individually. Besides, you can't love a crowd, but you can love one at a time. In order to do this we have care teams that walk the hallways, aisles, and seats to shake hands, hug, converse, and warm things up on Sunday mornings. We have greeters at all our doors. We encourage staff, singers, and musicians to walk the seats before and after services. We are bringing back name tags! What? Name tags?

I know what you're thinking ... "Ughh, name tags!" We're using the stick-on kind and writing people's first names on them. Everyone wears them. Members, attenders, and guests. There is definite power in being able to say hello to someone by name. People feel loved and valued when this happens. So often I've felt the adverse affect when I couldn't remember someone's name. Most people understand my dilemma of trying to remember hundreds of names, but there's still a tinge of defeat within an individual when I can't and a spark of joy when I can. It's those silly little, pesky little name tags that help us say hello by name.

Our staff also does exhaustive followup each week on new people in order to love people one at a time. Each week our staff dedicates time to writing at least 5 notes and making five phone calls as a part of our followup process. I'm always amazed when I walk into someone's house and see a note from our staff or myself that is plastered to the refrigerator. That note was sent months ago, but the love and value remains.

It's so easy to focus on the crowd, and many churches do. It's much more effective to focus on individuals. We are finding that as we love people one at a time, they add up after awhile! What new, trendy church-growth strategy can top this?

Our focus is also on feeding people the Word of God. I'm confident every church wants to do this, but we are getting very intentional with our efforts. We have a goal of giving someone the complete Word of God if they give us four years. In four years time, we hope someone who is a part of ACC will have been exposed to the entire Bible. That would be an awesome legacy to attach to our ministry.

In trying to feed people the Word, we have moved forward creatively. We put NIV Bibles under our chairs and tell people they can have a Bible as a gift from Antioch. We have spent a lot of money buying Bibles and giving them away, but this is a really good thing to spend our money on ... don't you think?

We also started doing the Bible wave. In similar fashion to what baseball fanatics do at a major league baseball game, we do in church. On a typical Sunday morning, I will say, "Get your Bibles out ... " and with that, someone on one side will stand up with their Bible and let out a "Whoooee!" This generates a wave of people and Bibles that ripples across our auditorium. Guests are usually a bit freaked out, but we explain that we are excited about God's Word and so we have become the first church in southern Indiana to employ the Bible wave. The Bible wave always wakes people up, cheers people up, and gets all the Bibles out and warmed up so people can be fed.

Rick Stedman says well-fed sheep are healthy, happy, and reproductive. In fact, the first function of a sheep to stop during times of famine is the reproduction process. Isn't that amazing? So why aren't many churches growing? Why are so many Christians unhappy and unhealthy? Maybe it's because they're just not being fed the living and active Word of God.

Lately, my sermons have shifted from being mostly topical to being more expository (one main text and verse by verse). We understand more and more how deeply people's lives are changed by God's Word, and not my words about God's Word. Rick Stedman's mentoring words to me were: "God did a really good job on the Bible. We should use it!" We do, and the hunger, growth, happiness, and healthiness have increased as well.

Next steps at Antioch are also unfolding as we purposefully try to connect people to God through prayer and worship. We know people want to be connected to other people when they walk through our doors, but we are convinced new people are coming to church primarily to connect with God. These days we are intentionally trying to pray more than we plan. Our staff meetings have turned into two-hour prayer meetings. Our elders meetings consist of 45 minutes of prayer and 45 minutes of Bible study as this leadership team tries to shepherd ACC through the ministry of prayer and the Word. These days we are pushing people to fill out prayer requests cards on Sunday mornings. These cards are for the people filling them out and for the people they want to invite to church. Each week we are getting inundated with hundreds of prayer requests that are then divided up among our staff and prayed over regularly. Talking about God is not enough. Our goal is for believers and seekers to experience God through prayer and worship.

Finally, our "next levels" goal is to creatively motivate people to pray for and invite their friends to church, and to serve our community. We have been privileged to be a part of an incredible movement of God. But movements can come and go. Movements ebb and flow and even stop. Nobody around Antioch wants the movement to stop. Our goal is to turn this movement of God ... this God thing ... into a revolution that never ends. Praying for and inviting friends, and serving our community has the makings of a revolution that will continue 25 years after they've placed me six feet under.

As we begin to develop creative ways to love people one at a time, feed people, connect people to God, and motivate people to reach out and serve, our anticipation remains high. We know revolutionary results can be things like: a natural outreach, constant growth, regular assimilation of people into ministry, and a church that is Biblical and healthy. Who wouldn't want to be a part of a church like that?

Sounds fairly easy doesn't it? Love, feed, connect, and motivate. That's it. That's the four-piston engine capable of driving our church to next levels. We still have our values and vision and process in place. Many of the God thing things we did in transition still serve us well today. However, God seems to be directing us back to His church-growth basics to position us to reach a post-modern generation that seeks basic truth.

So what's next? Who knows? It is a God thing after all. Maybe we'll go to a third service. Perhaps a Saturday night service would attract a different crowd of seekers. Who knows ... we might even expand Antioch into having multiple sites around the county and even in different states. What about church planting? Who knows ... that's the beauty of a God thing. It's all up to God.

There are some who demand we put a detailed, five-year growth plan in place. Maybe we should. Honestly, I struggle looking a year down the road because God things seem to be ever-changing and always risky. Although that may seem uncomfortable, a deeper level of security comes from knowing it's all in His hands. It's a God thing. Antioch continues to be a church the Lord delights in. We stumble and fumble, but we are being held firmly in His hands. It's all about God, and not us.

Although I write this book from my personal perspective, this God thing in a cornfield has certainly NOT been about the pastor. For some reason God chose me to play a small part in all that has taken place. I believe it would have happened with or without me, but I'm glad it included me. If God's hand would take me else where, I'm confident His hand would remain here as well. How unbelievable is that? I'm in for the ride, but I hold on loosely. It's God's grip that counts.

So here's my final shot at wrapping all of this up. I would love for you to experience a God thing someday. Whether it's at work, on the playing field, in the big city, or in a cornfield, may God place you smack dab in the middle of a great, big God thing. That's my prayer and hope for you. When He does, enjoy the ride!

[1] Taken from a message given by Bill Hybels at a Willow Creek Prevailing Church Conference.

[2] Warren, *The Purpose Driven Life*, (Grand Rapids: Zondervan, 2002), 171-178.

[3] Steven Curtis Chapman, *Heaven in the Real World*, Sparrow Records, 1994.

[4] McLaren, *the Church on the Other Side*, (Grand Rapids: Zondervan, 1998), 25.

[5] McManus, *An Unstoppable Force*, (Loveland, CO: Group Publishing, 2001), 80.

[6] Strobel, *Inside the Mind of Unchurched Harry & Mary*, (Grand Rapids: Zondervan, 1993), 224.

[7] Barna, *The Index of Leading Spiritual Indicators*, 50.

[8] Strobel, *Inside the Mind of Unchurched Harry & Mary*, (Grand Rapids: Zondervan, 1993), 190.

[9] Taken from a 1956 speech by Martin Luther King Jr., *Facing the Challenge of New Age*.

[10] As sung by Greg Ferguson, written by Scott Dyer, *A Place to Call Home*, Willow Creek Music.

[11] Warren, *The Purpose Driven Church*, (Grand Rapids: Zondervan, 1995), 66.

[12] Ibid, 49.

[13] Lowry, *Remotely Controlled Video*, (Word Inc., 1996).

[14] Audio Adrenaline, *Lift*, Forefront Records, 2001.

[15] Hendee, *A Peace Treaty With God*, Standard Publishing, 1984.

[16] Hybels, *Rediscovering Church*, (Grand Rapids, Zondervan 1995), 180-181.

[17] McLaren, *The Church On The Other Side*, (Grand Rapids, Zondervan 1998), 102.

[18] Taken from a seminar by Rick Stedman at the Loving People One at a Time Conference, Roseville, CA, Adventure Christian Church.

ACC

Membership Covenant

Having received Christ as my Lord and Savior and been baptized, being in agreement with ACC's vision, mission, purpose, and values, I commit myself to God and the other members of Antioch to do the following:

1. I will protect the unity of my church.
… by authentically loving other members.
… by refusing to gossip.
… by following the leaders.

2. I will share the responsibility of my church.
… by praying for its growth.
… by inviting seekers to attend.
… by warmly welcoming those who visit.

3. I will serve the ministry of my church.
… by discovering my spiritual gifts, talents and passions.
… by being equipped to serve.
… by developing a servant's heart.

4. I will support the vision of my church
… by attending faithfully.
… by living a Godly life.
… by being a part of a small group.
… by giving regularly.

Signed: _____

Date: _____

Printed in the United States
28717LVS00001B/188